WHITE ETHICS
AND
BLACK POWER

WHITE ETHICS
AND
BLACK POWER

The Emergence of the West Side Organization

WILLIAM W. ELLIS
Northwestern University

ALDINE PUBLISHING COMPANY
Chicago

First published 1969 by
Aldine Publishing Company
529 South Wabash Avenue
Chicago, Illinois 60605

Second printing, 1970

Library of Congress Catalog Card Number: 77–75046

Designed by Chestnut House

Printed in the United States of America

CONTENTS

v

PREFACE

In schools and colleges, in magazines and newspapers, on television and in public speeches, we are told that America is the world's most democratic nation, where all have an equal chance to enjoy material abundance, where all are respected equally, where poverty and oppression do not exist. Sometimes questions are raised about how closely America fits this rosy description, but the answers usually state that only slight adjustments need be made and offer no fundamental criticism. Racial oppression, poverty, the tendency toward a garrison state, and the other evils of American life are seen as minor problems, not basic negations of the enchanting image of America so often put before us.

The plain disjuncture between the ideal America and the reality is so great that serious voices among blacks, students, and others now challenge the ethical substance of the nation. To many blacks, the white ruling class of America no longer can say what is right and wrong and certainly can no longer tell blacks how best to pursue their liberation. This feeling is so strong among the adherents of the new militant movements formed under the political symbolism of "black power" that they have altogether revoked the ethical license of the white ruling class at the intellectual level. These new movements will bargain and contend with whites, even work closely with them for many purposes, but always with suspicion and caution.

The leadership of the black revolt is becoming more diverse as a result of these new forces. Once the province of the black middle class, it is increasingly invaded by those closer to the black masses. The social reformism of the integrationists has been joined by a strong new assertion of the tradition of black nationalism.

Like many intensely local political organizations emerging in urban black America, the West Side Organization—WSO—represents these trends. My concern here is with the nature of the leadership of WSO, which recognizes that blacks in America are a people with a distinctive culture and heritage who must build a common future out of their shared past. But the careers and outlook of the leaders, as representatives of what is new in the black revolt, are more important to this book.

Once successful criminals, the four major leaders of the West Side Organization have become successful community politicians. The image of the criminal in American life is often glamorous, particularly as shaped by Hollywood film makers. But the black criminal has never been glamorized. While white Americans easily believe that white criminals run vast organizations in the underworld, they view

black criminals as mindless villains. Yet Eldridge Cleaver
and Malcolm X, both criminals by ordinary definitions, have
become successful ideological leaders; it is stunning that the
leaders of the West Side Organization have made essentially
the same shift in their lives.

But who is the black criminal? Impoverished black communities consist of people unable to succeed by the normal
career routes open to most white Americans. Their failure
is not so much their own problem as it is a result of the workings of racism and class discrimination in American society.
They are uneducated and unskilled, and the dynamics of
their condition prevents them from becoming so. Many are
willing to take considerable abuse from racist employers to
get jobs as unskilled laborers. Those who are not must pursue criminal careers, at which only a few succeed. Among
the black poor, many proud and socially skilled men are professional criminals.

Many blacks see these activities merely as necessary for
survival, and to be sure, there are a few who engage in
criminality for the sport of it. But some blacks see criminal
acts as conscious acts against the social system, as rebellion,
even as revolution. It is not a long way from black criminality to political action. If a black criminal begins to view his
work as rebellion against the social order, and if he sees it
against a decade of overt black revolt, it begins to appear
counter-productive. Most black criminals rob and injure
other blacks; to be plainly revolutionary, their acts should
be directed at the powers that be. The enemy is diffusely
defined for the potentially revolutionary criminal as aspects
of the social order; for the converted criminal who is a re-
former or revolutionist the enemy is more explicitly defined
as those who oppress the black community.

Black criminals who become politicians bring skill to their new careers. It takes sensitivity, intelligence, and guile to become a successful criminal, not only ruthlessness. At least as much as a businessman, laborer, or clerk, they also have had to know who controls what and how in order to succeed as criminals operating in an ordered social context.

Yet there are some requirements of a new urban political organization that these men cannot fulfill. They must turn to black professionals for outside help; and the leaders of WSO have turned to whites as well. If white people want to help build the West Side Organization into an entity that can eventually become the government of Chicago's Near West Side, they are welcome. The relationships between leaders of WSO and white people who work closely with them are strained, but so are relationships with black professionals from outside and among the WSO men themselves, though for different reasons.

The tension between black and white requires no explanation. That among the leaders of WSO is relatively simple: suspicion often exists when strong personalities try to work together in exceptional circumstances. But the tension between impoverished leaders and the black intelligentsia deserves special attention. The two groups live under different kinds of oppression. And while the condition of each is known to the other, they understand these conditions differently. A bizarre conservatism has developed among certain black intellectuals, who see themselves as Americans and integrationists and judge black culture an unimportant subcategory of American culture. Leaders close to the black masses, on the other hand, have strong anti-intellectual elements in their thinking that are partly a reaction to the conservatism of some prominent members of the intelligentsia. The nonsensical description of the black community as a pathological social entity is confronted by the meaningless celebration of immediate action and analytically empty railings at the power structure. This gap must be closed. The present generation of the radical black intelligentsia must analyze the conditions under which blacks live and their relationship as a people with white America, and must create a broad-gauged vision of the future. They must articulate these thoughts in a way understandable to leaders closer to the black masses. These leaders in turn must develop an appreciation for the importance of analysis, planning, and ideology to inform their action. Cooperation will lead to better thinking and better action, and will increase the chances that the movement will succeed.

Those who report to the world at large on organizations in social movements have a different problem than those black intellectuals whose major audience is the black community. Social scientists and journalists in America generally operate under an ideology-laden code of professional conduct that requires objectivity. Only if you have no commitment to the people studied, it is argued, can you tell the truth about who they are and what they are doing.

But this objectivity is in effect a commitment to the ruling class. For it does no good to "report" conditions in the black community. Those who oppress will continue to do so. The ruling class wants intellectuals, especially social scientists and journalists, to be uncommitted to the black community and other rebellious groups. No commitment, no intellectual leadership for the revolution, no revolution. The ideology of uninvolved objectivity has effectively neutralized the intellectual class in America. Black intellectuals are separated from the new elements of leadership of the black movement, and the American intellectual class as a whole is the servant of those who rule.

Black intellectuals must provide intellectual leadership for the movement; white intellectuals, always under black guidance can make an important contribution to this work. Of all the intellectuals, social scientists and other students of society can make the most valuable contribution. They can perform three kinds of services:

(1) They can analyze the current operations of organization in the movement, providing leaders with accurate readings of the effects of their actions. Leaders need to know whether a rent strike, a boycott of the polls, or a street rebellion is getting the desired results. This kind of research requires access to an organization's plans, and of course no analyst could conduct such work or make it public without the explicit consent of its leaders.

(2) Investigators can conduct strategic research. They can analyze national and international social systems in order to inform action. They can construct alternative strategies and programs for change. On the basis of sound social analysis, they can prescribe and recommend.

(3) Finally, black intellectuals can create and articulate ideologies for the movement—views of the future rooted in past experience but going beyond it. These visionary constellations of values and goals should be closely related to the work of evaluation and strategic research. Ideology can become a powerful engine of the movement, but if it is not designed carefully and scientifically it can be disastrous.

University-based social scientists, faculty and students alike, have done little of this kind of work. Certainly they have written on what is wrong with America, but most often their audience has been the establishment or other social scientists, not those who seek major social reform or revolution. There is room for disinterested social analysis, but if American social scientists are to contribute to improving human life they must outgrow their celebration of objectivity and overcome the present reward structure of the American professions.

The nature of some new elements in black leadership and the need for some changes in the spirit and performance of American social science are the major themes of this volume.

Jane Taylor, Virginia Stewart, and Charles Baer brought patience and skill to the tasks involved in typing and proofreading the manuscript. Their assistance was made possible by the Northwestern University Program in Law and the Social Sciences.

WHITE ETHICS
AND
BLACK POWER

PROLOGUE

About a Very Few Men

This is a social science essay about the West Side Organization, an independent black community organization based in the Near West Side in the heart of metropolitan Chicago.

But it is really about the lives and ideas of a very few men—the leaders of the organization. Most of us who inhabit the quiet and prosperous parts of American cities would consider these lives exceptional, though in the context of America's ghettos of race and poverty they are not. These men have done many illegal things in seeking to come to terms with a brutal and even diabolical environment; it is not important that these acts are considered criminal, only that they enabled these men to survive, and even to succeed.

Success, usually defined as achieving high status with respect to one's fellows, applies to these men, even though they are poor and black and occupy the bottom rungs of American society. They have survived the challenges and threats of a hostile world and have emerged strong and independent human beings, unafraid to make commitments, not apologizing for themselves. They have lived through violence and deprivation, sickness and confusion, with death and profound despair their frequent companions. But they have survived.

They are exceptional in the context of American society as a whole, for few of us have been subjected to these pressures, but from another perspective spawned by another context, they are not exceptional. In the vast nation of the poor and black—at the heart of American society, yet separate from it—these men are heroes. What we fail to see is that the hero is often distinguished not by his creation of new values, but by his articulate celebration and embodiment of old ones. Heroes can be distinguished by the fact that they are supremely ordinary. As heroes, the leaders of the West Side Organization embody the hope and the beauty, the life style and the humanity, the destiny of the blacks in America. To study them and their thinking is to study all who are black in America, for the lives and thoughts of these heroes are the most readily available expressions of hopes for self and nation, of identity.

I do not mean to suggest that these men are celebrated—in America, in Chicago, or even on the West Side—for that would be to romanticize and distort their lives and reputations, to brutalize them. But they are heroes nonetheless, because there are many, many others like them. It has been impossible for black men in America to have any widely revered heroes save those designated by the whites who control the apparatus of communication—the publishing houses, newspapers, electronic media, and schools—by which heroes are made, by which men who are essentially common are made into potent social symbols. If blacks had heroes by their own designation, some would be men like the leaders of the West Side Organization.

The perspective that these men, and the community of American black men, have on American life and social analysis is different from the perspectives familiar to us in most popular and social science writings. While the WSO leaders admit that there may be such a thing as society, their major concern is with the quality of the day-to-day dealings individuals have with one another. And in their consideration of these dealings, they refuse to think in stereotypes and categories, except as these stereotypes and categories affect the ways individuals view themselves.

Theirs is not the reassertion of the kind of individualism that has been a major theme of American social history, the individualism that instrumentally pits man against man and class against class. Rather, it is another kind of individualism realized only through the most profound human commitment, that commitment born of the deepest, most beautiful, most complex, and most terrifying concern that one human being can have for another—put simply, it is born of love.

"Love" has been so romanticized in American popular culture that I use the word only with great hesitation, realizing that I run a great risk of being misunderstood. For love, as I view it, is an immensely complex and confounding relationship between individuals. It has nothing to do with agreement or commonality; it has everything to do with deference; it is central both to peace and harmony, and to violence and discord. Its essential quality is closeness and understanding. It is possible, therefore, quite literally to love one's enemies, though one may have to murder them. Love is simply engagement.

This book is about what some of the leaders of the West

Side Organization have to say and do about engagement, about love, about America, about mankind. What these men have said and done is very important to us, for these things summarize and illuminate the nature of the ancient and continuing American crisis. The lives and thoughts, the successes and frustrations, of these men form a compelling and constructive criticism of contemporary American life.

I have contrived this essay from this criticism—from the lives and thoughts of a few men who are poor and black (and of a few of their white associates). Fundamentally, the essay does not belong to me, but to them: the thoughts are theirs, the acts are theirs, and the criticism of American society is theirs. I have served only as a translator. No translation is perfect, however, and all of the shortcomings of this volume are my responsibility, and mine alone.

Many who live in America have been captured by the recent insurrections in and near the black communities of many of our cities. Buildings have been burned and looted by members of the lower classes—black, white, and brown. Police and armed forces have occupied these communities when they are black. Studies—like the Kerner Commission report on civil disorders—have been undertaken; and politicians and private citizens alike have asserted the need for massive programs of aid or repression for the black men and women of America.

The West Side of Chicago has had its share of this attention. There were insurrections in the summer of 1966 and again in the spring of 1968, following the assassination of Martin Luther King, Jr. But when the desperate have mounted programs of destruction and confusion, they have been less intense in the immediate area served by the West

Side Organization than in other parts of Chicago. This is no accident, but the result of the dedicated and dangerous work of the West Side Organization. In the summer of 1966 staff members went out into the street and persuaded the citizens of their community to stop their rebellion, while in other quarters of the city armed intervention by the military was required to stop the destruction. In 1968, on the evening of the King assassination, a crowd of about a thousand young black men gathered outside the office of the West Side Organization. The question they put to the leaders of the WSO was not whether they should burn up the shops and offices of business and professional men from the suburbs. Rather, it was what should be burned and how. The leaders of the organization talked the angry crowd away from its mission. While many limited sections of Chicago were leveled, no substantial insurrection took place on the Near West Side.

But all this is only incidental to what I have to say in the pages that follow. Forestalling insurrection is not the most important thing the West Side Organization does, nor does it constitute the meaning of the organization. There is no immutably noble purpose in stopping urban insurrections, when violence is practiced against the men, women, and children who are poor—and especially if they are black—by many of the rest of us each day. There is no necessary virtue in stopping the minor lootings and burnings of our lower-class insurrections when to many the whole of America is a permanent insurrection against the human spirit. Yet from the riots it is clear that WSO leadership is trusted and followed by important segments of the Near West Side black community.

Many of us have been captured by the recent urban insurrections. Certainly many in Chicago have been captured by them. But little has been done peacefully to change the conditions that have spawned them. Though reports have been written and commissions have been formed, the only change I can see is in the increased determination of the police and the armed forces of state and nation to "control" future disturbances.

During its entire history the West Side Organization has experienced many disappointments and defeats, together with its many victories. But during the last year or so the disappointment has become more intense. Following the West Side riots of 1966, the U.S. Office of Economic Opportunity, the national "war on poverty," invited the West Side Organization to submit a community development proposal. This invitation was met with jubilation by the WSO staff. The proposal was finally submitted the following April to begin programs in June 1967. For more than a year there was no definite response from the agency one way or the other; to date they have said neither yes nor no. In the meantime, the West Side Organization has turned to other social institutions in its quest for ways to fund its community development efforts, and has entered into an agreement with the Shell Oil Company that makes WSO the manager of a local gas station, the profits to be shared by WSO and Shell.

Taken together the results of these two experiences are ironic. It is well known that the Shell Oil Company, like many large-scale American commercial enterprises, has substantial business in the Union of South Africa, a factor that would seem to make them almost natural enemies of WSO. It is presumed that the agencies of our national government are likely to produce some substantial amelioration of the many dimensions of the American crisis. Yet in the past experience of the West Side Organization the government has been disappointing, while the Shell Oil Company has been a good business partner.

But our attentions in the current domestic crisis have been riveted on preventing riots, rather than on producing relationships like that between Shell Oil and the West Side Organization.

Unlike the oversimplified programs for community improvement that provide more jobs, better welfare payments, better public housing—more of the same things we are used to seeing, the things that have failed in the past—the relationship between Shell Oil and the West Side Organization provides the community with a "piece of the action." It is this slant on community development that has grown out of the disappointments with government agencies and out of the organizational style and intensely personal concerns of WSO. For this kind of community development provides the poor—and especially those who are poor and black—with some notion that they can be part of American life, not simply the servants or objects of it. And this has everything to do with what poor men and women think about America and about themselves.

Incidentally, this kind of development can stop riots, for it can provide the West Side Organization and other organizations like it with a factual basis for their appeals to the young to wait a little longer before they revolt. But only massive change and a new commitment from many quarters of American society to the realization of American values in fact as well as in rhetoric can ultimately save the nation from continued catastrophe.

This report on the West Side Organization is incomplete.

It does not tell all about the men and women who lead WSO because many important aspects of their lives—their sex and drinking habits, their mental and physical health—are private and have no place in these pages. Besides personal matters, certain facts about the organization are left out because they are private. For example, when WSO has been broke, it has paid bills with personal loans and other transactions that are important but not public information.

This book may be called incomplete in another way because it does not describe the ward and precinct politics of the West Side. Certainly WSO is a political organization, and West Side politics is important to it. But it is redundant to give the usual descriptions of politics in the urban black community because this politics has been discussed and pondered for many years in publications and public discourse under the title "problems of the cities." Several books could be written about WSO's efforts to deal with these problems: about efforts to improve the quality of police administration on the West Side, about efforts to change urban renewal plans, about dealings with the Democratic party, about WSO's long persecution by the Chicago legal system. But anyone with good sense and an interest in city politics knows many such stories; they are common. The Kerner Commission report, hailed as a courageous reassessment of the condition of the lower classes in urban America, is nevertheless boring.

More than that, the Kerner report and other studies like it are an escape. Many in America have come to believe that the revelation of evil will cause it to disappear in the strong light of our discussion and concern. But our discussion and concern are as old as the oppression of the lower classes in American cities, as old as American cities themselves. The evil continues in spite of the fact that it has been described many times in American history.

Any rich or powerful man who has ever thought about why he personally does not want any real live black revolutionists or others among the oppressed in his house, on his block, in his corporations, in his governments, schools, textbooks, histories, in his mind—knows what the government of the West Side is about, for he is its governor in his attitudes, actions, and comportment. He has read the Kerner report and chuckled, for he has known its findings all along; he has made them. Those who already know how America is ruled—and especially, how its blacks are ruled—include the rich and powerful who have bothered to think about why they do so well while others starve in fat America, and many blacks and other oppressed peoples as well. Those who do not know how America is ruled do not want to know. And that is why I have left out the facts of West Side politics called for by the tradition of political writing in America: they are already known by everyone who wants to know them. By-passing these facts, I give the beginnings of what may be done to change the way America is ruled in this interpretation of what is essential and new in the West Side Organization.

Furthermore, it is dangerous to describe West Side politics. While everyone who has thought seriously about America knows how it and its "West Sides" are ruled, not everyone knows the details of how this particular West Side is ruled. To point to structures, to name names, to reveal the illegal acts by which the West Side is ruled, is to challenge the gangsters and politicians and businessmen of the West Side elite, and WSO is not quite ready for that. The challenge will come later, when WSO has found the means to keep its leaders and members from being enslaved or destroyed by the political establishment in Chicago.

But in spite of the omissions, this is an intensely political book because it tells how one group of oppressed men and women define politics, and how they have tried to change their political situation. The definitions of politics implied by the oppressed people of WSO are different from most textbooks and journalistic definitions.

In the chapters that follow, the difficulties in understanding the West Side Organization are detailed in Chapter 1; the life histories and thoughts of several WSO leaders are presented in Chapters 2 and 3; Chapters 4 and 5 deal with some essential facts about the milieu and workings of the West Side Organization; some common thoughts on social action in the interest of the poor are discussed in Chapter 6; and the WSO perspectives on racial oppression, American society, and social analysis are revealed in Chapter 7. Concluding thoughts are given in the final chapter.

PART

I

INTRODUCTION

1

UNDERSTANDING WSO

What follows is an exploratory study, which is another way of saying that it was initially undertaken without a clearly defined research design, but with the notion that its chief result would be some knowledge about what questions should be asked of social configurations like the West Side Organization in future researches. This is not to say that I began with no ideas, with no notions of what to look for and of what to ignore.

My initial interests in WSO were very simple. At a suburban meeting of some middle class friends of the organization, I learned a number of things in a conversation with Eugene Harris, an official of the organization, that compelled my attention. First, it was clear that the West Side Organization was controlled by black people in a black community in which the material conditions of life are as bad as in any urban slum in America. Second, it seemed that the men from the West Side Organization present at the meeting were intelligent, articulate, and aggressive, though only one had been educated past high school. Third, Harris told me a bit about the spirit of the organization: he said many of its staff members had given up their jobs to work for a meager salary in the organization. He said the organization was "their religion." He described the head- quarters as run-down, but open and congenial to people on the West Side. He told me a bit about the dispatch and efficiency with which the organization handles its business. But perhaps the fact that I was most taken by was that these were *men*, not the usual young students and middle- aged social reformers who have carried many such organi- zations in the past, but strong, confident, intelligent black men who had begun to speak and to act politically on their own behalf.

I found all of this very interesting and sought first to work for the West Side Organization and, ultimately, to explain it to others.

The Inadequacy of the Usual Methods and Techniques

To explain adequately the West Side Organization, it is important to indicate how I know about it so that the reader will not be entirely at the mercy of the assertions in this re- port. This knowledge is especially important and difficult in this study because the ways of knowing—methods and techniques of research—usually employed by political scien- tists are not adequate to learn about the West Side Organi- zation and similar social configurations.

The usual *methods* (overall research strategies) utilized

in the approach of modern political science to the social world may be characterized by the preoccupation with objective social realities. The scientist is primarily concerned with describing a given situation in terms of how *he* sees it; and even when he is concerned with how *participants* in a situation view their lives, his efforts are to describe their world in his (the scientist's) terms.

The *techniques* of data collection usually employed by political scientists are really quite restricted. Though most of the major data collection techniques that have been employed by the greater community of social scientists—including sociologists, psychologists, anthropologists, and others, as well as political scientists—have at one time or other been utilized in political research, only a few of them have been widely used in the studies reported in the literature of contemporary political science.

Foremost among these are the techniques making up the research operation known as the sample survey. Usually in a sample survey researchers select respondents from a group of people on a chance basis, with the notion that by studying a "sample" of a group, they can economically make generalizations about what the entire group thinks, feels, or does with regard to the subjects around which a given inquiry is centered. They design questions aimed at eliciting responses from the selected individuals that will become "data" representing the behavior of interest. The questions are tried out on a few individuals in a "pre-test" to provide some notion of how the questions can be improved—that is, how they can be sharpened to elicit the desired kinds of responses, and to allow interviews to go smoothly. Then interviewers are trained to administer the questions, and finally, the questions are asked. In a sample survey national in scope the administrative task is enormous; the communications necessary to insure that the questions are being asked in a uniform fashion of all subjects are extensive. The data—responses to the questions—are ultimately compiled in a central place, analyzed, and brought to bear on the research questions central to the project.

The sample survey has been utilized to provide answers to many different kinds of research questions—from how best to market a new brand of cigarettes to how best to market a new presidential candidate. Though the techniques are remarkably flexible, providing many possibilities for researchers with divergent interests, with the dramatic increase in their use since World War II and their consequent reporting in newspapers and slick magazines, they have become familiar to the public mind and, unhappily, stereotyped in it as well. Recently, I was quite alarmed to discover that the students in one of my undergraduate courses, who knew next to nothing about social science, had some very clear ideas about what constituted an adequate sample survey, and indeed about what constituted an adequate social science. Clearly the source of their beliefs about social science and about sample surveys was not their previous training, but their experiences as participants in the mainstream of American culture, which apparently carries these notions and imprints them on the young. The sample survey, narrowly construed, is thought by many Americans to constitute the only adequate basis for a technology of social science. Most other techniques are considered, at best, shoddy.

The basis of the sample survey is the interviewing of a fraction of a group of individuals selected on a chance basis. Many inquiries utilize interviews of groups of individuals who are *not* selected on a chance basis. These may either provide for the interviewing of entire populations (for example, an entire state legislature), or for the selection of interviewees on the basis of some outstanding characteristics (for example, madmen of different kinds, to explore the extreme cases in abnormality to elucidate the normal).

All these techniques of data collection are based on the interview—that is, on *asking* individuals what they think and do, and how they feel.

Another set of techniques of data collection is organized around the *observation* of individuals—that is, *watching* what people do. Important works have been based on participant observation, where the reporter was a party to the scene he describes. These include works by presidential assistants about their days with their great man, and by those Presidents themselves about their days with their great assistants. There are also accounts, usually more illuminating, by participant observers who are merely visitors to the social goings-on they report. Among these are the reports of political anthropologists who study political life in societies vastly different from our own in parts of the world that have simpler technologies than our own, like African or Asian tribal or peasant societies, and those of some students of social movements, like religious revivals or revolutions, who are never quite captured by the movements they study. These reports may in part be based on informal unstructured interviews, if the workers who conduct them are given to asking questions that are relevant to the inquiry without being relevant to the social interaction in which they are involved. For example, a presidential assistant whose assignment is to keep the President informed of foreign developments may, in the course of his daily work, ask the President—and others who work in the White House—questions about how they reached certain decisions or how they view foreigners. But the extent to which one is involved in the social situation he is observing, and whether he asks questions irrelevant to the social processes being observed—these factors are not central to the basic differentiation of questioning and observation as techniques of data collection. No matter what the nature of a given observation study, it still rests on the notion that the researcher is watching what people actually do, rather than eliciting reports on what they do, as is the style of the interviewer.

But it should be clear that the distinction between these two techniques is blurred when they are not opposed as stereotypes. The stereotyped interview involves the researcher in asking highly structured questions of interviewees. But as the interview becomes longer and less highly structured, the researcher becomes substantially involved with his subjects. The stereotyped observational research strategy involves the researcher in simply watching what his subjects do. But as he watches less and engages himself more in the social situation being studied, he too may become more involved with his subjects. In this gray area between engagement and disengagement the ambiguity in the distinction between interviewing and observation asserts itself.

Other techniques of social research are variants and combinations of these two fundamental strategies, but the penchant of modern political scientists has been to dwell on techniques near the stereotypes of the two major strategies in their work. The usual sample survey interview is close to the ideal interview, while the utilization of reports of social events appearing in newspapers (and extant social science literature) is close to the ideal observation.

WHY THE INADEQUACIES?

If a political scientist undertakes to study individuals significantly different from himself in the way they look at the world, his questions and observations, if close to the stereotyped usage of these strategies, may be greatly misleading.

If there is a gap in social status between the scientist and his subjects, responses to his questions and the behavior presented to him for observation by his subjects are likely to be distorted. All but two of the individuals who are my concern in this study are of lower social status than myself. Because of this difference, if I questioned and watched them without engaging them, they would answer and act more in accordance with the way they think they should answer and act in the presence of a person of higher social status than they would in the exclusive company of their fellows. This gulf between the middle class social scientist and the poor *black* man makes understanding the condition of the poor (and of the poor and black) extremely difficult. An appropriate analogue to this difficult relation is the suspicion with which the natives regard the social scientist who is viewed as the emissary of the colonial authorities. The natives tell the colonists and their emissaries what both colonist and native expect in the expression of deference of the native to the higher social status of the colonist. What the native thinks of the colonist may be obscured to the colonist and even to himself because of the status differential.

Second, the native who knows his own mind may "put the colonist on." If the native is oppressed by the colonist —that is, if the colonist steals much of the native's material wealth and attempts to steal his pride as well—he confronts the native as a figure of vast power. If the native is unwilling to believe that he is inferior, he will not permit the colonist to divest him of his pride. And if he is unwilling to murder the colonist or drive him away by force, then to insure his mental survival, to shield his own personality from a basic threat, he must involve the colonist in a series of *games*. These games are designed by the native, consciously or unconsciously, to lead the colonist to believe that he is being deferred to, but in the native's mind and those of his fellows, they render the colonist foolish and without humanity.

Such games are known in American slang as a "put-on." Through its use the natives survive. In America many black people are crushed by the oppression to which they are subjected. Many, however, manage to survive—to maintain some self-respect, some semblance of ego strength. And like the natives who survive, they do it (in part) by putting white people on. For this reason, I believe that a lot of the empirical work by American social scientists on the attitudes and activities of black people may have been misleading. If some white social scientist, or his Negro emissary *qua* interviewer, asks a black person a question, however carefully designed, the response is likely to be either (optimistically) what the black person believes is appropriate to say to the white man (or his emissary) in the interview situation, or (at worst) a clear put-on.

Finally, given these two formidable barriers to understanding, as a social scientist I opt for the strategy of the involved (even partisan) observer. I am a member of the West Side Organization and have done a modest amount of work for it—not a leader, but a kind of technical adviser.

In the initial stages of my study I faced the quandary of all partisan observers—the intense conflict between my role as a partisan of WSO and my role as a social scientist. After a certain time spent in a social situation, a partisan observer becomes confused. He is uncertain of what is being revealed to him as a reporter and what is being revealed to him as a friend. He may find that one resolution of this conflict requires him to consider himself a subject of his own study, perhaps the most important subject. And in the ensuing mental contortions he may find that he is going mad.

The hesitation to become fully involved with, to become fully committed to, those who are initially thought of as subjects for study may damage both the research report and the researcher.

The usual ways of knowing applied to the social world by political scientists are inadequate in studying WSO, and even the strategy of partisanship presents problems.

My Posture toward
the West Side Organization

The resolution of these problems is critically important to this study. Only in their resolution was there to be found a way of knowing—a *method* of research—about the West Side Organization that provides adequate description and explanation.

IMMANUEL KANT AND THE PUT-ON

In his two major works Immanuel Kant laid the philo-
sophical cornerstones of two trends in modern social science.
The first of those trends, exemplified by the work of Émile
Durkheim, applied Kant's scientific outlook in the examination of man as an object. The other major trend, seen in the
work of Florian Znaniecki and others, applied Kant's moral
perspective in the examination of man "as a personal being,
seeking to study man's values."[1] As I said before, the first
of these two perspectives is deeply imbedded in the substance of modern political research, directing our view to
the objective realities of human existence through the use
of research tools that maintain our distance from the men
we study. If, however, we keep our distance from those who
are significantly different from us, in no way can we come
to understand them except as they allow themselves to be
understood in terms of our view of them. For this reason
black men in America have been regarded by social scientists as inferior white men, as men sharing all the values of
the mainstream of American society, but who, because of
"unequal opportunities," are almost universally of low socio-
economic status. Baldly stated, this is the perspective of the
imperialist, who in his preoccupation with himself is unable
to judge others, even in his most charitable moments, except
by his own standards.

In no way can modern social science come to understand
the American black man (or his antagonists, for that matter) from the posture of disengagement—that is, from the
posture which requires that its practitioners study and judge

1. Severyn T. Bruyn, *The Human Perspective in Sociology* (Prentice-Hall, 1966), pp. 165–166.

American black men in accordance with their own values. For these values, the value configuration of Americans, one remembers with both anguish and enlightenment, have permitted, and even sponsored, more than ten generations of the oppression of black men in this land.

All of us, black and white, are creatures of these values in that we are all socially trained to speak of freedom and equality and at the same time to explain away the ugliness of oppression. If the system is believed to be an open one, it is easy to accept the assertion that all deserve what they get. In this way, both black and white have come to believe that whites are superior—for they have earned their status in a free society, while blacks are inferior—for they too have earned their status without restraint. In American life the black man is confronted with a monstrous view of himself, and in many circumstances can respond only by the put-on or by violence if he is to have any hope of maintaining his sanity.

In trying to understand blacks in contemporary America, the *scientific* Kant—not the *humanistic* one—would be put on or slapped in the mouth or both.

SIGNIFICANCE FOR THIS WORK

This study would provide little illumination if it merely used the most popular approaches of contemporary political science. I would then simply present myself as a social scientist interested in learning about the West Side Organization. And undoubtedly I would be put on, much in the same way I would put on a social scientist who presented himself as a student of my self. I act as a partisan, which in fact is not a distortion or ruse. In this role, I am not so much put on, but am treated the way members of the West Side

Organization leadership group treat outsiders who offer their intensive help. This is not to say that I am not ever put on, only that I am less put on than I would be otherwise.

I am not oppressed in the same way or to the same degree that poor black people are, but I know from my own experience something about the thoughts and strategies of the oppressed. So I was prepared for the preliminary games and tests they subjected me to, because I have used them on others myself. And I was aware that coming to know an oppressed man is eased, but not accomplished, by the simple presentation of oneself as an ally instead of as a student come to pick over an unusual variant of mankind.

I too am a black man. Many black men have come to the black poor not as brothers but as welfare officials, policemen, school teachers, and clergymen who have treated them perhaps even worse than have white people. And this history makes the game more difficult for me in some respects than it is for a white man. Any black man who stayed "in the system" long enough to become a licensed professional is immediately suspect, because undoubtedly he has had to suffer indignities unknown to most white people. And in the course of this wretched passage, many such men have come to believe that they are respected by white people—in spite of the indignities they have suffered. And believing themselves to be respected by white people, they come to hold some of the same attitudes toward the blacks who are their less fortunate cousins and brothers as do white people. So the man of professional status—a man like myself—who tries to present himself as an ally to impoverished black people is necessarily suspect.

But the poor and black are confused by such a presentation. They are reassured and even ecstatic to see that blacks are capable of becoming professionals, but at the same time they are wary of black professionals who present themselves as partisans because of the long history of evil dealt them by such people.

My relationships to the West Side Organization are extremely complex. All of us in the organization find ourselves involved in games that would make three-dimensional chess seem like tictactoe. But what is important is that we are engaged with one another. And the reason that we can spend so much energy dealing with one another is that we know the game is not of our own making. Our separation has been shaped by American society, a society that victimizes us all. And though this is never stated explicitly—for that, too, is a part of the game—it is a fundamental understanding extremely difficult to come by, but which merits its high price.

I have resolved the problem of the conflicts between my role as partisan and role as social scientist in a simple but difficult way. I have abdicated my role as social scientist *qua* the disengaged man for the role of *partisan as social scientist*. This change was made consciously, because it is personally and intellectually the only way I can deal with WSO.

The intellectual trappings of modern political science do not permit the analysis of oppression. Only if the social scientist is willing to engage the men whose lives he reports does he earn the possibility of gaining insights into how they see the world. But he runs the risk of being driven mad if he is not prepared for the put-on.

SIGNIFICANCE FOR CROSS-CULTURAL WORK IN GENERAL

My work on the Near West Side of Chicago has been cross-cultural; the individuals I have studied and worked with are participants in a way of life somewhat different from my own. Their language is different, their kinship patterns are different, their technology is different, their ways of dealing with one another are different, their religions are different, their world view is different. We are black, a bond of enormous importance, but I was both black and poor only during childhood, while they have been so all their lives. I have had one small advantage over many—both black and white—who have tried to study urban black people, the fact that I went to the West Side with a substantially less well-developed notion that black people are evil and ignorant. This notion is inculcated in us all in American society—white and black. And it was not by accident that I avoided this. When I was very young both my parents worked hard every day to help me avoid this part of American citizenship training. And though I did not escape this training entirely, my mind has the hard kernel of belief that black people are fully equal to whites in mental and physical endowments, which has made it possible for me to entertain the members of the West Side Organization as equals from our first acquaintance.

I am convinced that this kind of belief is not easy to come by, and this conviction has serious implications for the training of social scientists. If it is not possible for those who would become social scientists to avoid the restrictions imposed on their views of others derived from the powerful socializing forces of society, how can they possibly ever come to understand others whose ways are different from their own? For to become a part of a society is to develop a self that is fundamentally linked to that society—a self that must be defended from threats at all costs. Such threats are very much a part of the confrontation between self and other incurred in seeking knowledge of the subjective realities so fundamentally a part of anyone's social world. Unless a social scientist can survive these threats—and, ideally, not find a substantially different social self threatening—it is unlikely that he will learn much about those who live differently from him.

Methods and Techniques Used

Anthropologists customarily utilize that special combination of interviewing and observation known as participant observation. They go to live with people who are different from themselves for extended periods of time, then write research reports about what they believe to be important facets of their lives.

I have been a participant observer among white people in America for more than a quarter of a century. They are different from me, and I have studied them closely, talking with them (in interviews) and observing their behavior. I have written no reports of these researches, but this is the only part of the anthropologist's cycle which I have not been through.

I did not at first consider myself a participant observer; I had considered myself a full participant in American society. But as early as primary school I realized that the white children—that is, most of the children—in my classes and neighborhood treated me as something special, as an outsider. It soon became apparent that I could not be as close to them as they were to one another. But because I would remain among them for a long time, I had to develop some strategy for dealing with them. This strategy is essentially to adopt the posture of the participant observer: remaining keenly aware that I am an outsider, while engaging the white world so that I would get along and become educated, a strategy that enabled me to develop clear pictures of white people both from my own perspective and theirs.

My personal history was constantly before me as I considered what research strategy to utilize in seeking to come to grips with the West Side Organization. Well-schooled in an informal way in the strategies of participant observation, and dedicated to WSO from the outset, I began to work on finding out about WSO in several ways.

THE INTERVIEW AS CONVERSATION

First I talked to people who were instrumental in starting and in developing the organization. Reverend J. A. Hargraves, one of the founders and now president, was especially helpful in providing background information on how the organization was founded, its history, and the sources of the organizational style of WSO. Another early interview was helpful—a conversation in the park over beer with William Darden, director of WSO's Welfare Union. Darden and I discussed our views on the nature of the problems of black people in America, and what would be required to "solve" them. It became clear, as we talked on for some time, that here was a man of extraordinary abilities and intelligence. The man's style of looking at the world and his intelligence made this conversation an excellent preface to other interviews with West Side Organization people that were to follow. In subsequent conversations with others in WSO I began to discern the style of each man in viewing the social world, and to understand the intelligence—even the social science—that underlay that style.

In the summer of 1966 I interviewed many members of the West Side Organization. Some interviews were more or less structured attempts to develop life histories of key people. Others were casual conversations about whatever was on our minds at the moment. All the interviews were not really interviews as we commonly understand them, but informal conversations. They were conducted in the organization's central office, on walks, in demonstrations, in parks, in bars, during automobile trips. In no case did I ever present myself as a social scientist, but as a friend and partisan. I told everyone I interviewed that I was writing a book about the West Side Organization, and I made it clear that anyone interviewed could look over statements about him in the manuscript to check their accuracy and to delete what he did not wish to be published.

Everyone was very kind and open to me in all our conversations, though from time to time we found ourselves involved in some of the games I described earlier. They seemed candid in talking to me about their lives. At other times I have found that in conversation people almost universally portrayed themselves as something other than they really believed themselves to be. I never got that impression in my conversations with these men and women. They described themselves as neither superhuman nor incompetent. In my experience that is extraordinary.

Though I have held conversations with WSO leaders frequently ever since I have been associated with the organization, two sets of interviews were directed at specific research objectives. I have already mentioned the opening interviews with Darden and Hargraves. These became part of the first major set of interviews, in which I sought to develop life histories of a few of the key leaders. These were

completed in the summer of 1966. The second major set of
interviews was conducted in the spring of 1967. I had
learned much from the life histories and from other conversations with members of the West Side Organization. But
it became clear as I looked over my data and notes in the
winter of 1966–67 that while I could construct a world view,
intelligence, and social science of WSO from these materials,
I would have had to write what I thought about the views
and lives of the WSO leadership, rather than reporting its
own statements and simply translating them into terms
comprehensible by social scientists and others who have not
shared the experience of being poor and black. I also felt
the need to run a check on what I thought to be the facts
about the structure of the organization's leadership.

Therefore, the second major set of interviews was aimed
at producing data that would allow me (a) to be a translator of the views and lives of the leaders of the West Side
Organization rather than an interpreter and (b) to refine
my thoughts on the interrelationships of the leaders. Though
a more carefully organized interview agenda was used to
structure these conversations, the interview was still more
conversation than interview.

OBSERVATION AS ENGAGEMENT

In the years I was doing the research for this book, I
spent more than two hundred hours in meetings, in which
the officers of the West Side Organization participated, and
simply sitting in the WSO central office observing how individuals dealt with one another.

In most of the meetings I was a participant, an advisor,
a counselor, but in no case did I take a major part in deter-

mining what the organization did. But sometimes I tried to convince people to do things, though I was always cautious in doing this.

In the meetings and in my observation of behavior at the WSO main office, I consciously tried to see how other participants viewed the interaction in progress. This was not so difficult when I simply sat and watched. But when I took an active part, I became preoccupied with how *I* viewed the interaction, and with how *I* could help shape the discussion. In one way this tendency posed an obstacle to my understanding how others viewed the developing situations. But in another way it created an intuitive understanding of how my associates viewed things, that which usually results only from dealing with men in some common cause.

These dealings have included: meetings of the WSO staff, meetings of the highest councils of civil rights organizations in Chicago, staff meetings evaluating the work of staff members, meetings of the Committee on Community Organization of the Chicago City Missionary Society (a major source of funds for WSO), meetings with city officials, meetings to resolve the Cicero crisis of the summer of 1966,[2] and many meetings of WSO officials with people in their neighborhood. This wide variety permitted me to see the men in action in many settings. By examining their changes in style from one social setting to another, I was able to get a clearer picture of the nature of their intelligence and social skills.

2. In the "Cicero crisis" many blacks in Chicago civil rights organizations threatened to march through the town of Cicero, known for feelings of intense hatred for blacks, if an open housing agreement and other provisions of concern to them were not enacted by the local government.

THE USE OF OTHER PEOPLE'S DATA: THE KEATING LOG

Donald Keating was one of the clergymen who helped to organize WSO. He was a traineee at Chicago's Urban Training Center for Christian Mission (UTC), a new Protestant institution devoted to training ministers of diverse denominations for work in the deteriorating centers of America's great cities. Keating was assigned to the development of one of the training bases for the UTC, social settings to which trainees could be sent to learn first hand about some of the problems of modern urban life. This particular training base was to be located on Chicago's Near West Side, and was, as originally envisioned, a union of the unemployed. Keating, Robert Strom, and one or two others were given the assignment of developing this project. Strom has become a major participant in WSO over the years. He is mentioned again in the chapters that follow.

Keating and the others traveled through the neighborhood, trying to learn about the way of life there. At an early stage in these activities, Keating took the assignment of keeping a record of important events. Though he was not trained as a social scientist or journalist, he managed to capture many useful impressions of meetings, of confrontations with officials of public and private organizations, and of what it is like to develop independent political organization in an American urban slum.

The Keating log is an accurate and responsible source of information about the early days of WSO. I have not used it without criticism and qualification; every statement used in this study was checked in interviews with other participants in the early work on WSO.

Strengths and Weaknesses

This strategy of openly partisan participation was the most appropriate way of setting about the work of helping and understanding the West Side Organization. While it is true that in immersing myself in the organization, I have lost the perspective permitted by social and psychological distance from other human beings, I was freed from the psychologically debilitating role conflicts that would have resulted from any attempt to be objective about the West Side Organization. Indeed, objectivity would have required me to separate myself from the West Side Organization and all its aspirations and problems. And since I came to the organization with many of the same aspirations and problems, this separation would have required me to examine myself as an other, that is, to engage in a kind of forced alienation.

Because I tried to look at the world as the West Side Organization looks at it, I was (and am) able to feel the coherence and strength of its way of life, where it is like mine and where it is different.

PART

II

THE LEADERS

2

CAREERS

This chapter is concerned with the careers, the life histories, of some of the major participants in the West Side Organization.[1]

To a very large measure this informal presentation is the most important part of this essay. Among other things, it begins to answer the critical question of why these men, many of whom had been engaged in criminal activities, made the decision and the sacrifice to work for WSO when they could have achieved wealth and status by going with the organizations that are currently major powers in the Near West Side ghetto, the political and criminal syndicates. The answer is intimately linked to issues in the study of social change, for on the individual level, the choice of

1. The life histories and other data on leaders of the West Side Organization set forth in this chapter were gleaned from informal unstructured interviews conducted during the summer of 1966 and the spring of 1967 (see Chapter 1).

these men, black and white, to undertake the kinds of activities which they have in WSO *is* social change. In setting out information on these decisions, this chapter essentially sets forth the data for the study and, therefore provides the substance of the remainder of the argument in following chapters.

I have purposely told more here than I use in the analysis appearing in later chapters—to portray my friends in dimensions required by friendship but not by analysis. But I have not included detailed psychiatric or sociological data, nor have I presented extensive tabulations of character or environmental traits of potential relevance to the discussion. Set forth below are the stories of some WSO people and some propositions that could serve to structure more detailed studies. It is not possible for me to tell everything I know about these people. Their family lives and religious involvements, their personal habits and weaknesses, their fears and frustrations—all these things are relevant to their political activity in the West Side Organization. But this essay is not a group confessional, and only a few facets of the lives of these people are revealed in this chapter. To respect the privacy of the men and women of WSO, I have stressed only those facts and judgments about them that I believe most important in explaining their successful involvement in the organization.

Chester Robinson, Executive Director

A man in his late thirties, Chester Robinson is slightly below average height, and fat. But he is not one of those fat men who walks unconfidently and whose manner conveys dismay at having assimilated so much of his environment. He has light brown skin and very dark brown hair.

Ordinarily he is not very talkative, and often sits at his desk for long periods working through stacks of papers, or reading a book or newspaper, with only an occasional remark to those around him. But when he does talk, it is friendly banter with others, if no work is in progress, or strong and articulate phrases revealing a keen intelligence (even though he has a very slight speech impediment). When he talks, he looks at others with a directness that commands attention and respect from friends and enemies alike. He is often aggressive and dominant, but not brutal, to those around him; heated argument is a favorite activity of his. But when nothing is happening in the office, no business or important argument, he likes to drink brandy and watch television. He is an easy man, strong and candid; yet, as in other leaders of WSO, there is an uncompromising and unapologetic strain of the bully in him.

Robinson was born into a large rural family in Tucker, Arkansas, in 1931, the third eldest of a family of nine children. His father's family—of eleven brothers—had a sizable farm, and most of them lived and worked on it. They spent most of their time in the country and seldom went into town, which limited the interaction they had with whites.

One day Robinson's father went into town alone to purchase supplies. He was accosted by several drunk and surly white men, who began a malicious conversation with him that rapidly became a fight. Large and strong, Robinson's father soon drove the men away, seriously injuring one or two of them.

A few hours after he got home that evening a group of thirty to forty white men arrived at the farm, demanding that he, now a criminal by local norms, be surrendered up to them for punishment. But the other ten Robinson brothers, Chester's uncles, refused—guns in hand. The posse departed, but, it was learned later, immediately began to round up a larger group. The next day the Robinson brothers were warned that several hundred men would be coming to the farm that night to demand again that the offender be surrendered to them. Chester's family left for Chicago immediately, though his uncles and their families stayed behind. During the next several months the remaining brothers and their families were continually harassed and finally after Chester's grandfather sold the farm all of them moved.

When Robinson's immediate family arrived in Chicago, they took up residence in a one-room single-story dwelling. It stood between two buildings several stories tall, and one day when there was an explosion in one of them, a lot of rubble fell on the Robinson household. One of Robinson's brothers was killed, and everyone else was injured. The somewhat less than generous settlement the family received from the landlord amounted to $300, a neat quantification of the value of a black child's life in America.

After this tragedy, his father—who then had a steady job with a trucking company—began to drink wine heavily, the cheapest available "effective" alcoholic drink. He went to work after a time for the Works Progress Administration, then went on relief, and finally was totally on state aid.

Robinson began school when he was five, attending a trade school that was only 30 per cent black. By the time he reached the seventh grade he was known as a troublemaker, and he transferred to another vocational school for "bad

boys." His reputation made it difficult for him at home because his older brother and sister were model students,
which may have been part of the reason for his problems
in school. His program consisted . of academic studies in
the morning and vocational studies in the afternoon. Care-
ful attendance was not kept in the afternoon, so Robinson,
then fourteen, left school at noon and worked delivering
coal.

When he graduated from grammar school, the vocational
school for bad boys, Chester Robinson transferred back to
his original school, only to leave when he was 15 after an
altercation with the principal. His memories of the final
school are unpleasant. He remembers teachers making fun
of him, especially of the patches on his clothing. He remembers fights with other students. He remembers little
joy or interest in learning. His last several months in school,
Robinson worked the night shift (11 P.M. to 7 A.M.) in a
steel mill. When he finally quit school, he worked on a junk
truck for a year or so at $10 a day. The job had been given
to him by the father of a close girl friend, and it ended
when his friendship with the girl ended. He was to have
married her, but they fought, he struck her, and they parted.

His attachment to her had been deep, and he began to
brood, finally turning to wine when he learned that she
had married someone else. His depression deepened, and
when decent jobs became scarce, placing severe limitations
on his ability to earn a living, he took to smoking marijuana.
Marijuana smoking is not a constant companion of despera-
tion, but some people—like the Chester Robinson years ago
—do it because it eases their unhappiness. As his consump-
tion of marijuana increased, it became widely known in
the neighborhood that he carried it with him most of the

time, and people began to come to him to buy. After a
time, his trade in marijuana grew to such proportions and
profitability that he quit his job to sell it as his exclusive
livelihood. He became the leader of a small gang whose
members stole hubcaps from automobiles and engaged in
other petty thievery. He was in jail for several short periods
for fights, and in 1953 he was arrested for the unlawful sale
of narcotics. In this first major encounter with the authorities he was acquitted.

Everyone engaged in illegal business in lower class communities for any length of time must work out an affiliation
—or at least an understanding—with the organized criminal
syndicates. As Robinson's career developed, he was charged
with other responsibilities by syndicate executives, among
which was "picking up policy"—collecting bets for a gambling operation similar to the numbers racket. At the peak
of his career, he was making several hundred dollars a day
and was known in many parts of Chicago as one of the
city's biggest dealers in marijuana. Meanwhile, his older
brother and sister were becoming other kinds of professionals—his brother a truck driver and his sister a school
teacher.

He spent most of 1955 in jail on a narcotics conviction.
When he got out, he collected eleven hundred dollars in
debts owed him and got a job as a janitor in a movie theater
through one of the criminal organizations. He settled down
in this new job and steadily saved money toward getting
married to a new girl friend. A bad break came when he
was sent to jail for a four-year term on a narcotics conviction for a crime he did not commit.

In jail he did two years of high school, attended barber .

college, and read extensively. He had felt guilty since childhood because of his poor academic performance compared
to his older brother's and sister's. Motivated by a sense of
intellectual inadequacy, he took the opportunity offered by
his confinement to increase his knowledge and understanding of himself and the world about him. Concentrating on
philosophy and history and the Bible, he spent hours thinking about the condition of American black men and his own
place in society. Quizzed closely on the nature of the readings, he reveals only general changes in his thoughts; the
most striking was his new detection of similarities in the
pattern of oppression suffered by minorities in many societies.

He was released from prison in the spring of 1961 a year
early for good behavior, and returned to the West Side
where he went to work as a barber. He continued his reading, now concentrating on black history, and taught an informal course in this field to a group of about thirty adolescents under the auspices of a local church. In 1964 he
took up with WSO, recruited directly by the initial participants in the organization, who had heard about him through
his reputation as a teacher. It was a logical step, from studying and teaching the history of the achievements and
oppression of black men America to working to increase
these achievements and end this oppression.

Asked why he works with WSO, he says that he does not
know the answer, or that the answer is too complex to bear
expression; he claims never to have considered the question.
He states that he had done wrong for so long that he felt
obligated to atone for his sins by trying to help others with
their problems, as he had tried to help himself with his own.

He says that his mother had lost faith in him during his criminal career, and that he is working for WSO to return to her good graces.

William Darden,
Director of the Welfare Union

William Darden is known by his friends as "Thirsty." He is small, lean, dark brown, and has the build and gait of a former high school halfback. His face is round and mobile, frowning in intense concentration or opened in quiet laughter. Its only stable feature is an abundant black moustache.

Darden is an active and often nervous man who finds it difficult to sit still. He travels tirelessly all over the city in his work, and is aggressive—when appropriate, even hostile —in his style of doing business. He will sit quietly in meetings for a long time, then in the speech of the black community press a point with great drama, persuasiveness, and eloquence. He is in his early thirties, married, and has three children. His children are very important to him. He is not apologetic about his own life, but he often speaks of his dreams for his children, hoping that their possibilities for achievement will be better than his were. He pays close attention to their lives—their thoughts and health, their worries and excitements. His hope is more for them than for himself.

Darden was born in 1935 in Franklin, Tennessee. His mother and father were never together, and his siblings share only his mother as a common parent. Beginning school a year late and losing a year on account of illness, he did not graduate from high school until he was twenty. Darden did well in school, earning an overall B average and several perfect attendance citations. His athletic activities won him four football letters and one basketball letter; and when he was a senior, he had several offers of athletic scholarships to colleges.

He says that he has never been able to stand threats and insults, and he was in many fights in school and after. During his mid-teens he began to gamble and was arrested, convicted, and fined on four occasions for this activity while still in school. These and other incidents combined with difficult financial circumstances in his family to keep him from going to college.

Among these incidents was a shooting. After a summer working in a pea cannery in Rochester to save money for college, he returned to his house to find that his mother had been beaten by a man who had been a friend of hers. Consumed by rage, he took the family gun from its hiding place and began to look around Franklin for the man. When he found him, the man denied the charge altogether, but Darden, still very angry, demanded that he confront his mother, and drew his gun. The man edged toward him and continued to do so in spite of warnings to remain still. Darden shot him, then went to his aunt, from whom he borrowed some money, intending to go to Chicago where his father was then living. He got as far as Nashville before deciding to go back and turn himself in to the police. He was convicted of "shooting in a public place" and sentenced to 30 days in jail and a $50 fine, but was released after only three days in jail on the intercession with the police of family friends. The incident was not, according to the police, to have become a part of his permanent record, but somehow it did—a fact that was to cause him considerable grief later on.

He returned to school the same month, but the hope of going to college was soon abandoned. After graduating he took the alternative to college that many young lower class men of his age take—he joined the service, enlisting in the Air Force in 1954 for a four-year term, with the idea that he could make a fortune gambling, as have others in their careers in the armed services. He gambled heavily in the Air Force, and won much of the time. When he enlisted, the recruiting sergeant asked him if he had a record, and Darden replied by relating the shooting incident to him. The sergeant said this would not affect his application for enlistment or his military career and that it would not be included in his record.

But after he completed advanced training in teletype school, his record was examined carefully, as were those of all other applicants, and the shooting incident was revealed.

But the consequences of this record were not made clear until after his Christmas leave spent in Franklin, during which he was involved in another shooting incident and also got married. At the end of his leave, he and his bride learned that his clearance for cryptographic school was not going through—that his vocational future in the Air Force was severely limited.

At the end of January 1956 there was a minor uprising of enlisted men on the base. It was not a race riot, but it developed racial overtones for Darden when he had an encounter with a white sergeant from Alabama who told him that he would be discharged from the service for insubordination because Darden talked back when the sergeant manhandled him—this in spite of the fact that Darden had not been an active participant in the uprising.

Darden was court-martialled in February, charged with falsification of his enlistment papers despite the earlier promise, and told that either he accept discharge as an "undesirable character" or go to Leavenworth prison.

When he was discharged from the Air Force in April 1956, he and his wife went to Chicago, where he secured a job as a laborer in a soft-drink bottling plant. He remained with this firm for six-and-a-half years, finally being laid off because he refused to accept a reduction in seniority. It was then April 1962, and his wife was expecting their third child. She had worked as a packer at a mail-order house intermittently from 1960 until the spring of 1962. Darden began looking for another job, but was unsuccessful because of his service record. He earned some extra money by gambling because the unemployment insurance checks he received from the state simply were not enough to make it for a family of four. Finally, in February 1964 he and his family went on public assistance till March 1965, when Darden went to work for the West Side Organization full time. He participated for a short period in a metalworking training program financed by the federal government, but did not finish it because it was poorly taught and participants were required to work with inferior materials. He found the program insulting and a waste of his time.

Darden's career until he joined WSO had periods of steady employment and stability, but its greater themes were of the violence and deprivation of the streets. His life was tense and uneven—affection for his wife and children and violence in his living in the street life. He always carried a gun, his life was frequently threatened, and he was often a half-step from prison. But at the same time he worked as a professional gambler at night, he also worked at legitimate pursuits by day—first in the Air Force, then in the bottling plant in Chicago, then in a government training program.

He first come to WSO in August 1964 to seek an adjustment of his other than honorable Air Force discharge because it was keeping him from getting a good job. He had known Chester Robinson and William Clark before. As Darden learned about what Robinson was doing and of the great change that had taken place in the lives of both Clark and Robinson as a result of their participation in WSO, he gradually expanded his involvement in WSO, becoming totally immersed in it during the Centennial Laundry crisis. Following this, he worked for a time with Reverend Donald Keating on housing violations in the neighborhood. In January 1965 he started working for WSO weekday mornings for a part-time salary. Later on he worked full time handling welfare grievances, and ultimately became the Director of the WSO Welfare Union.

Formerly, his way of dealing with others in disputes had almost always 'been violent, but since his work in WSO he has acquired abilities to express himself articulately, even brilliantly, and to achieve many of the outcomes he desires without resorting to violence. He is an expert in the techniques and psychology of interpersonal violence. And he has sometimes spoken of the way that violence tends to consume those who practice it as an integral part of their lives. He has not lost his nerve, nor is his expertise in violence tarnished. He is still very aggressive, but his aggressiveness has taken new forms.

William Clark, Director of
Welfare Union Local

An old friend of Robinson's, William Clark was born on Chicago's West Side in 1932. A large friendly man with dark brown skin and well-kept "processed" (straightened) hair, he is clean shaven and usually wears sunglasses. He is a hard man to know and unwilling to talk much about himself. At times he is easy—most of the time, speaking of his "love for mankind." And in fact he does enjoy people, does love mankind. But often he falls into fear and suspicion—most often suspicion of the motives of white people doing business with WSO. Like Robinson and Darden, he led a violent life before joining WSO.

He was the youngest child of a family of nine children, and he speaks of a father who did not realize that he had any talents until he was twenty-seven years old. He is reflective about his life, is embarrassed, and says that there is nothing to tell. He quit school in the sixth grade because he found his studies uninteresting and irrelevant to his perceived future—this at the age of fifteen or sixteen. From then on his career consisted of menial jobs, constant swindling, occasional stick-ups, and prison. He went to jail the first time in 1954, and remained there two years serving sentences for assault, robbery, and the illegal possession of narcotics. He went back in 1955 for violation of probation and armed robbery, this time for sixteen months.

When he got out, he picked up his former way of life and was arrested in 1959 for a crime he did not commit. He was acquitted in a trial presided over by a judge who made a deep impression on him. The judge, he says, was the fair-

est one he had ever had. He apparently persuaded Clark
to quit his career as a professional criminal by provoking
him to consider his life. In his thoughts, Clark reflected on
all of his boyhood friends, most of whom were dead, in jail,
or addicted to narcotics. He saw himself as having been a
little more fortunate than they, and decided to quit his
profession, though he continued to make his living by petty
swindling.

He married in 1960, and soon after went on public assistance for a few months; he had more or less left the street
life but could not find a job.

Like many others, he wandered into WSO headquarters
off the street in 1965 to visit friends, in this case Robinson,
whom he had known for twenty years. In early conversations with Robinson and Darden he abused the organization,
calling it a "front job for the white folks." Gradually, however, he came to see that he was mistaken, and he became
a full-time worker. He now heads one of the Welfare Union
locals.

Clark became a part of WSO because his friends were
in it. And like the major leaders of the organization, he is
an expert in violence and in the ways of the streets. He has
much stronger interests in sports and music than the others,
and he is one of Chicago's most accomplished softball play-
ers and is involved in many youth athletic programs.

John Crawford, Director of
Welfare Union Local

Born in 1939, the oldest child of a family of fourteen
children, John Crawford was brought to Chicago as a small

boy. The Crawfords lived on the West Side until 1951 or 1952, then moved to the other great black community in the city's south. He attended a number of grammar schools, changing as his family moved, doing reasonably well in each school. He was bored in vocational high school, and dropped out in 1957 when he was eighteen. After working in a pickle factory for about a week he was fired for a mistake that blew out all the lights. Though he had joined the National Guard two years earlier to fulfill his military obligation, he was drafted into active military service, and received training at Fort Sam Houston in Texas. He was released from service in March 1958.

He went to jail for the first time the following winter on a minor charge. In prison he went to school to improve his reading and writing skills and spent many hours boxing in the gymnasium.

With time off for good behavior, he got out in September 1959, but he was back in jail the next month for breaking into a dry cleaners. He was released in the spring of 1960, and after serving his two weeks' summer army reserve training he found a job. But he was called "boy" and otherwise patronized and humiliated by his bosses. From the time of his youth he was not able to accept this kind of treatment, and on all of the menial jobs he had before, he either got into fights or, as here, quit. He began to drink wine heavily and that winter became very ill with the internal disorders that commonly result from alcoholism.

Deeply frightened he tried for a few months to curtail his drinking. He speaks of this event as changing his life markedly; he began going to church again (as he had in his childhood), and he married in April 1961.

In May 1961 Crawford was ordered back into the army

for six weeks as a penalty for missing meetings of his National Guard unit. Following this period he got a job as a punch-press operator in a factory. Forced to work nights in order to keep his job, he was dismayed to find that there was a conflict with his military reserve meetings. His employer illegally refused to release him from work to attend the meetings, so he cut work one day to avoid another military penalty and was fired. He looked for work for a time without success, and, as have many other black men in the same position before him, re-enlisted in the army. He was sent to Fort Lee, Virginia, and his bride moved in with her parents in a housing project on the South Side of Chicago. While stationed in Virginia, Crawford made only one trip home—in March 1962, when his son was born.

Out of the service again in August, he resumed his pattern of an occasional menial job, unemployment and welfare. His family was back on public assistance in September 1963 and continued so until Crawford began to take training at the Allied Institute of Technology under a grant from a federal retraining program. He stayed in the program until November, learning to operate a milling machine.

In the winter of 1964–65 he became one of the original four West Side participants in the fledgling West Side Organization in the hope of finding employment through this new channel. He became so interested in WSO, however, that he stayed on as a volunteer and ultimately became a paid staff member. He is presently the manager of a local of the Welfare Union. Like Clark, he has held his job at WSO longer than any other job he has had. In addition to working long hours each day handling welfare complaints, he runs weekly open community meetings.

Three themes bind his life together: violence (resulting

from his inability to put up with insults), religion, and alcoholism. Up to about the age of 15, he says, he was very mild
and reserved, but then he became aggressive when provoked
—whether by black men or white. Neither Crawford nor I
have an adequate explanation for this shift. He is a large,
strong man over six feet and 250 pounds, and he won most
of his fights, even when he was attacked in twos and threes.
He seldom expresses his aggressiveness with his fists any
more but with words, and he is proud of the verbal skills
he has newly acquired—skills that enable him to handle
unpleasant welfare workers without resorting to heated argument or violence, skills at conducting intense arguments
with coworkers in WSO without resorting to violence. Indeed, his role in the in-house fights in the organization has
been that of mediator between those who would otherwise
probably part company.

His religious involvement occurred primarily during
childhood. Directed by a deeply religious mother, he and
many of his brothers and sisters went to church until their
teens. Crawford stopped going in late adolescence, but took
up again in his early twenties as part of an effort to pull himself together. He no longer goes to church, but in the weekly
community meetings he is very skillful in leading spirituals
and "freedom songs." He is a very good amateur gospel
singer and has sung in several groups on the West Side.

John Crawford drank his way through late adolescence
and into early adulthood—not for fun, but because it provided a momentary escape from the frustration of not being
able to find a job that would not humiliate him and from
his related feelings of worthlessness. Since he has been at
WSO he has severely curtailed his drinking.

Crawford is the youngest of the major leaders of WSO,

and he has intense anxieties about some of the conflicts in the organization, which occasionally cause him to withdraw for a day or so into the privacy of his personal thoughts. But his role is very important; he dampens conflict in the organization, helping to keep it from disintegrating. Queried about his future, he responds that he would like to make WSO or something similar his life work, for it is here at last that he has found his fulfillment and self-respect.

Patricia Stock, Editor of the *Torch*

Patricia Stock is white. It is monstrous that in mid-twentieth century America this has to be among the most important facts about her. What is more interesting is that she is a member of a conservative Republican family without being the kind of fugitive from another way of life most often found among white workers in black communities.

The oldest of three children, she has lived a quiet, easy life—the kind of life common to most people who live in white, middle-class, urban environments: she was religious and attended church regularly; she was studious and better than average in school; she was a good child and caused her parents no grief.

Until she got to college she had no interest in criticizing her way of life or in examining her mental insides to determine if this were the kind of life she was most interested in having. Her initial involvement in what might be considered unusual for her background was brief participation in a college endeavor to change the social rules relating to women students and rules banning speakers of radical political persuasion from the campus. She also read books of the new American "radical right"—particularly the works of Ayn Rand. She soon became disenchanted, though without going on to anything else—remaining dissatisfied with the life she had been leading and for which her future was tagged—the solid middle-class way of her parents.

Graduating in 1964 with a journalism degree from Elmhurst College, a small church-related school in a western suburb of Chicago, she worked as a reporter for a weekly newspaper in a Chicago suburb. She enjoyed the work, but remained dissatisfied. Her roommate somehow had learned of WSO and, in addition to her full-time job, tutored students at WSO headquarters in the evenings. Patricia Stock became interested in WSO, visited the Roosevelt Road office and later started to work up a newspaper for the organization on a part-time basis. Eventually she quit her job to work on the *Torch* full time.

Her role is peripheral to the major decision-making processes of the organization. Though she attends leadership meetings from time to time, she does not participate in them as an equal bearing a full measure of influence on what happens. She might best be characterized as a devoted journalist, bringing her skills to bear on advancing WSO, without participating in forming the grand strategies that dictate *how* WSO is to be advanced. The autonomous judgment she exercises in deciding what news to report and how to report it, and in soliciting advertisements with the *Torch*'s advertising managers, James Halsell and Erskine Jones, gives her large responsibilities for portraying the organization to the community.

But again, the most important thing about her is that she is white. The difficulties that have characterized the relations between whites and blacks in the West Side Organization, and that are common to all such working relationships, are dealt with in Chapter 4. She has not found herself as embroiled in these conflicts as others have because her part in making important decisions is not great. Yet she is trusted by those who do and accepted as a partisan of the causes of WSO.

She is deceiving in her apparent simplicity and naïvete. Seen on the street, she is taken for a young, middle class girl of suburban lineage: she wears no outsized earrings and uses little profanity—characteristics rarely found among young women who do unusual things in this society, whether they be career girls, political activists, or professional "hangers-on" of whatever color. She states flatly that she is not a revolutionist and her flamboyance is limited. But somehow her concerns for the shape of American society—particularly for the oppression of its minorities—are more convincing than those of Americans in flowers and beads.

Robert Strom, Chaplain and Organizer

Reverend Robert Strom is the WSO Chaplain and one of the original Urban Training Center participants in the formation of the organization. He, too, is white. He is one of the few white people to make contact on the West Side. He has not come as an emissary bearing the gifts of civilization, as so many others do; rather he is a human being from another culture, one whose members are responsible for the oppression of black men in America, and he has presented himself as an individual with skills who would help

them to do what *they*—the people of the West Side—wanted
to do.

Propositions

Chester Robinson, William Darden, William Clark, and
John Crawford are all men who have lived for a considerable time in the guts of Chicago's Near West Side; it is
home to them. And in their separate life paths, which have
been knitted together in the West Side Organization, one
finds important similarities and differences.

All have spent a lot of time on the West Side, and they
were well known to many in the community long before
there was a WSO. All four were regarded as exceptionally
tough men with records of violence. They have been members of the Near West Side elite longer than they have been
in WSO.

These similarities are quite telling. Since all these men
had experienced formidable blocks in their efforts to achieve
status by ordinary means—education and hard work at legal
pursuits—they turned at one time or another to extraordinary means, seeking to become respected by becoming
successful at pursuits that are common, but illegal, in lower
class urban communities. All were reasonably good at it:
Robinson was by far the most successful in his business as
a purveyor of marijuana, while Clark, Darden, and Crawford were somewhat less successful and prominent. Significantly, even though these men turned to what are criminal
careers by the standards of American society as a whole,
they did not substantially lose their ability to be warm and
kind to their friends.

The conclusion to be drawn here is simple, and may be stated as a proposition to guide further inquiries into organizations like WSO:

PROPOSITION 1

The only men who live in lower-class black communities likely to be successful participants in political organizations such as WSO, which use legal means to promote change, are those who have been successful in employing the illegal means required for success in the lower-class black community, but who have not become so alienated from their fellows that they can show no warmth and affection in their relations with them. This likelihood is enhanced by long residence in the communities that are the milieus of the political organizations in question.

Many black people are not aggressive men, for they have been crushed by society. Of those who are aggressive, only a small number succeed by utilizing the means prescribed by American society as a whole. Few are able to attain the levels of higher education and training required to secure good jobs and the concomitant status. Those who fail in such attempts usually turn to the other (illicit) means of achieving status prescribed by the way of life in lower-class, urban, black communities. Those who also fail in these pursuits either get killed, are sent to prison for extensive periods, or become addicts or alcoholics. Thus, almost all persons in lower-class black communities capable of being aggressive have had some success in criminal careers. Of these, only those who have maintained a capacity for getting along peaceably with their friends are able to participate in the give and take, in the argument and negotiation, of the ongoing business of organization life.

As for the differences between these men. Clark and Crawford were more alienated from their social surroundings than Darden and Robinson, and they had less formal (in Darden's case) and informal (Robinson's case) education. Darden completed high school in the normal way, and Robinson tutored himself in his prison reading. Crawford completed high school in an unusual way, in the army; and Clark dropped out of school at an early age. This leads to the second proposition:

PROPOSITION 2

Within the leadership structures of a lower-class black organization, leadership rank is positively correlated with education (formal or informal), and negatively correlated with alienation. (Education and alienation may or may not be related.)

Further, there are differences in the experiences of these four men in their dealings with human beings. Clark and Crawford had few business dealings—here criminal—that would have involved them in manipulating and controlling others. Robinson and Darden were different. Because Robinson sold marijuana he had to work with large criminal organizations in Chicago. As a professional gambler, Darden acquired formidable skill in manipulating small groups of men.

PROPOSITION 3

Within the leadership structures of a lower-class black political organization, leadership rank is correlated with

early experience in illegal activities that require administrative skills—in the broad sense of the ability to
manipulate others.

These conclusions are stated as propositions that may
serve for further inquiry but I have enough confidence in
them to use them as operating principles in my role as a
political actor.

The people discussed in this chapter have one major thing
in common, whether they are black or white, lower class or
middle class: they seem exceptional, they seem unlike their
fellows. The lower-class blacks are exceptional because they
have become effective political leaders on the Near West
Side, not in spite of their success as criminals, but because
of it. Their prowess in the illicit realms of social relations
had given them the ego strength and the social skills required to participate in the quest for changes in the condition of black people.

The middle-class people, Robert Strom and Patricia Stock,
are exceptional in that they are able to deal with people
of lower social status (according to mainstream perspectives) without patronizing them. Not many middle-class
people, black or white, are able to do this, though many try.

3

THE FRUITS OF EXPERIENCE

The experiences detailed in the last chapter have shaped
what the four black leaders of the West Side Organization
think about their world and their place in it—their world
view. These thoughts and views are critical to our understanding of their actions, for most men act and plan in a
framework of what they think of society. And since the
position of these men, and of other new political leaders
in the black communities of America, is critical in the
context of the present incipient social upheaval, what they
think as a framework for their actions is critical in understanding the nature of their style of leadership, and future
of the continuing American domestic crisis as a whole.

Thoughts on America and the World

The central outlook of the leaders of WSO on the American social world was best expressed by one of them in the

phrase: "They got it; we want it." "They" is most members of the middle and upper classes—including middle class blacks. These people are regarded with suspicion by the men of WSO because many encounters with them are unpleasant. Middle class people—who have more than they have—usually want something from them, either adherence to some religion, payment of some debt, their votes, their bodies, their lives. Some middle class people—sadly, more whites than blacks to date—present themselves to the men of WSO as friends and allies, and these few are not regarded in the same way as are others. To the leaders of WSO, notions of an enemy "they" are not strictly attached to race or class, but class identification is as important as race.

Second is "it": what "they" have got—a much richer material life than those who live on the Near West Side, and a hand in shaping their own destinies. Pleasant houses and apartments, good incomes, excellent educational facilities for their children, and extensive leisure are hallmarks of the affluent American way of life that the leaders of WSO want. The power to mold their own destinies—some control over the political structure and the productivity of their community—is also an American value they embrace. But other facets of the affluent way of life in America do not form part of the goal structure of these men. They do not aspire to the styles of dress and expression of the men and women of affluent America, nor do they aspire to the relative coldness of human dealings in those ways of life.

In the minds of WSO leaders, the country is white-ruled with the acquiescence, and even assistance, of many affluent blacks, and these people manage society in order to get the lion's share of what there is of wealth, prestige, and all the other things they care about. The men of WSO view the present organization of American society as consistently oppressing all blacks with a few exceptions. They come to this view through study and direct experience. They have read American history and traced the changing styles of American racial oppression. They have dealt with decades of ruthless oppression by white politicians and government bureaucrats who rule the black people of the Near West Side. America has failed them and oppressed them at every turn. They are committed—in the words of Malcolm X—to doing "whatever is necessary" to end it.

Third, who is "we"? "We" is the vast numbers of the black poor. The identification of WSO leaders is stronger with poor urban blacks in the north than with poor rural and urban blacks in the south, but the identification with other poor black people is very strong overall. WSO leaders generally regard northern urban black people as better off than those in the rural south: "Down there they have got people working for nothing—and no welfare either. Here at least we can make a little money when we can find work, and there is a little welfare money when we can't. Down there, too, the people are more afraid than here."

Malcolm X's influence is apparent in the thinking of the WSO leadership and summarizes their views of America and their place in it. Malcolm has been misunderstood by many white Americans and by some blacks as well. (So have other leaders, like those of WSO.) But what he said was devastatingly simple, and it had little to do with the ex- hortations to unprovoked violence by black people that have been wrongly attributed to him.

He said that black people have been led to believe that they are inferior to whites, a fact that is clear in the efforts of blacks to emulate whites in straightening their hair, bleaching their skins, and other acts of self-mutilation directed to make them look white.[1] It is also clear in the way some black people seek to associate with white people at any cost, even their self-respect. This has been true of many kinds of black people, but it is cast in the sharpest relief in the aspirations of many middle class blacks to occupy powerless positions as showcase executives in corporations, government agencies, foundations, and universities.

He said further that the black people have a great heritage that whites have tried to keep from them, a heritage of African kingdoms—some, political kingdoms; others, less formal realms of creativeness and art. He also maintained that the traditional, and even natural, religion of black men is Islam—(a part of his thinking that most black people influenced by Malcolm have not bought).

Malcolm said that black people should, in the realization that they are at least equal to white people in terms of their inborn abilities and heritage, band together to try to confront their white enemies. In the initial years of his national prominence Malcolm preached that brotherhood with the white man was impossible, exhorting black people to set themselves apart so as not to become contaminated by the white and his way of life, whose capacity for oppression he saw as limitless. Black people, he said, should not wish to be like whites because of the cruelty that whites have manifested toward black America and many other peoples throughout the world; they should not emulate such an example, he implied.

To men of honesty and clear vision of whatever color

1. For Malcolm X's thinking, see *The Autobiography of Malcolm X* (Grove Press, 1965), the first nine chapters and particularly pp. 42, 93–94, 162–163, 220, 251–252, 338–342.

or class, this is a persuasive argument, but many American whites have seen it as fanatical, for they believe that only a few of their fellows (certainly not themselves) have participated in the centuries of American racial oppression. Naturally no one wishes to take the blame for what has happened.

In the last several years of his life, influenced by the fundamental brotherhood he witnessed in the interrelations of white and black Muslims from all over the world, Malcolm came to believe that brotherhood between white and black was possible, a reversal of his earlier posture. Yet he never said that this brotherhood should be a goal in itself —only a desirable by-product of the struggle to achieve equality in material life and to promote cultural pluralism that would assure the maintenance of the best facets of the life of the black community in America.

Finally, he said that black people should try to achieve these goals by whatever means necessary. He never urged blacks to engage in unprovoked violence, but if nonviolence failed (which he saw as inevitable), the daily violence of police and others to black people in word and deed should be met by violence.

Not all the leaders of the West Side Organization have read Malcolm's speeches and autobiography in detail, nor can it be said that they are followers. Yet obviously their thought and outlook parallel his. They stress that black people are not inferior to whites, that black people have a rich heritage, that brotherhood with whites is desirable but that other goals are more important. On occasion they point out, as did Malcolm, that the spirit of affluent America— white and black—is corrupt and not to be emulated.

But Malcolm's greatest direct influence is as a model for

their individual behavior in the way he reformed and educated himself. Like the men of WSO, Malcolm was once a professional criminal and he spent much time in prison, yet he became an effective political leader. Like the men of WSO, Malcolm became expert in the techniques and psychology of interpersonal violence from his encounters during adolescence with street life in the black community; but as they became adults, both Malcolm and the men of WSO came to view violence as dangerous, unpleasant, and to be avoided—though not at the cost of freedom.

BEYOND AMERICA

Turning to a broader perspective: the thoughts of WSO leaders on international relations and other aspects of the world beyond America are not well developed; their primary concerns are intensely local. The only recurrent theme in their conversations is that the wars America has fought abroad—and the one it is presently waging in Southeast Asia—have been fought to defend a way of life that keeps them at the bottom.

While their present, but not unqualified, adherence to nonviolent tactics indicates some commitment to the American political order, the limits of their identification of themselves as citizens of the nation are revealed in their approaches to American foreign relations.

The way WSO leaders see America and their place in it is an unstable amalgam of limited belief in the fundamental correctness of the system and great dissatisfaction with their lot in it. They have limited optimism about the ability of America to accommodate the changes in their condition they are so earnestly trying to stimulate.

Thoughts on Themselves:
Efficacy and Alternatives

The WSO leaders discussed here are strong personalities with capacities for openness and for pressing their wishes on others--peaceably usually, but sometimes with threats. But on rare occasions all of them show signs of the intense insecurities characteristic of black men in America, a result of the mental torture of being confined to the lowest place in American society. For example, once in a while in the face of the different style of speech and intellectual manners of the more educated leaders of the black freedom movement, the WSO men are closemouthed and withdrawn. And when they are asked about their reasons for remaining still, they express a certain bitterness about not being able to understand persons with college degrees.

In spite of these occasional feelings of inadequacy, their general feelings of efficacy and competence are very high. All experienced some success in life, though it may have been in criminal work. People acquire feelings of competence from achievement in these kinds of activities just as well as they do in socially approved activities. In fact, these feelings of competence enabled them to undertake the work of WSO in articulating the interests of the Near West Side to the rest of the Chicago political system. Had they no feeling of efficacy in any area of human endeavor, as do a great many inhabitants of the black communities of America, they could not have possibly done this work in the organization.

All feel guilty about their past illegal activities, neverthe-less. This guilt helps explain their occasional sense of in-

competence when they are confronted with law-abiding
college-trained men and women, and their concomitant
feelings of great competence as leaders within the crime-
saturated ghetto. The difference in their feelings among
different kinds of people does not mean they are ineffective
speakers to affluent audiences; to the contrary, they are very
effective with such audiences.

In viewing their personal alternatives in life, they reveal
how their values differ from those of many other people in
American society. Each of these leaders is fully capable
of earning more than $150 a week (tax free) by swindling,
and some could make much more. At WSO the top salary
is much less. I believe that under these circumstances most
American men would go back to the street, for material
wealth is what enchants the majority of us. But the WSO
leaders have made great material sacrifices to participate
in the organization. Personal rectitude, self-respect, and the
rapid re-creation of their community are more important to
them than material gain. Political power, which they exer-
cise with skill in the Chicago political arena, is also more
important. At a great price they have for the present chosen
the alternative of legal political participation rather than
illegal activities as their road to achievement of change.

Thoughts on WSO:
Efficacy and Alternatives

The leaders of WSO emphasize nonviolence because they
believe it is presently the most effective strategic theme of
the available alternatives. The other alternatives are postures of unconditional and conditional violence. Taking a
strategic posture of unconditional violence would set them

against all else in the community save the black poor. Their tactics would consist of ultimatums sanctioned by assassination and by commando-guerrilla raids on the officials of government, business, and criminal organizations. Their offices and meetings would be secret, as would their membership lists, and their internal discipline would be severe. Taking a strategic posture of conditional violence, they would make demands and then carefully escalate the sanctions employed against their designated enemies in each crisis, the final sanction being some kind of organized violence. They might demand that policemen in black communities treat citizens with the same respect accorded to residents of other parts of town. At each firmly substantiated new report of police impropriety, they might issue a formal complaint to the local authorities. If the reports continued, they might beat up a few policemen. And if they still persisted, they might kill a few high-ranking police officers.

Both of these strategic themes have been the hallmarks of other social movements, most recently in the former colonial nations, and they may also become the hallmarks of the present black social movements in America before they go full cycle. The leaders of WSO are long-time experts in small-scale, interpersonal violence. And because of this —not in spite of it—they seek to avoid violence. To the present, they have been skillful enough and successful enough in other than violent strategies so that they have not had to use violence in their political work. These successes have given them enough confidence in the American political system to support their continuance of nonviolent strategies; but their support of the system is not unconditional, and the time may come when they will see violence as a necessity, the only remaining possibility.

Given the present nonviolent set of their perspectives on

action, there still remain alternatives for action and the necessity of choosing between them. The organization could have developed in the style of the political and criminal organizations that have ruled the Near West Side black community virtually since its inception. Leaders could have manipulated slum dwellers for their personal financial benefit, levying fines for noncooperation and taxes as insurance against violence. Or they could have learned the ways of politics in the suburbs and other more affluent parts of the metropolis. Or they could have organized themselves for the sole purpose of engaging in protest demonstrations of various kinds.

But rather than engaging in these familiar kinds of activities within the other than violent means that comprise the present strategy, they have creatively organized themselves as an agency of defense for the impoverished individual who is daily victimized by traditional community agencies—by governments, churches, and businesses. And they look forward to becoming an instrument for community development. They have begun negotiations with several corporations to begin community-operated businesses on the West Side. A Shell Oil Company gas station has already been opened under WSO management.

In the course of their work they have from time to time felt powerless and frustrated. These emotions are not primarily the result of feeling incompetent in dealing with city officials and other antagonists, but come rather from the persistent lack of funds to carry out desired programs. WSO complaints are not centered around the meagerness of salaries, though that is important, but around the limitations in office space and size of staff imposed by the organizational budget.

PART

III

THE WEST SIDE
ORGANIZATION

4

SOME FACTS ABOUT WSO
AND ITS WORLD

You will not find a full description of all facets of life on the West Side in this report, though that would be informative. Equally, I do not give a detailed description of the ultimate sources of the ideas of crucial importance in guiding the initial activities of the organization. And I do not present a history of the organization. Yet some part of these three things are important to this inquiry because they are significant links to the world outside the organization and help to place it in the social context of American life.

A Different World

Every city is comprised of many social worlds. Life on Chicago's West Side is very different from life in many other quarters of the city. (The South Side is largely black, but many middle-class Negroes live there, a factor that distinguishes it from the West Side, which is almost universally poor and black.) It is a way of life that is unknown to most people who do not live in the black ghettos of America.

The area known to compilers of demographic data on Chicago as the "Near West Side" is roughly coterminous with the area in which the West Side Organization has developed.[1] About 125,000 people live there, of whom a little more than a half are black. This fact is misleading, however, because there are substantial islands of white people in the center of the community, surrounding a large medical center, and near a new campus of the University of Illinois. The rest of the area is nearly 100 per cent black, and the boundaries between racial sectors are very sharp. Other enclaves in the community house people of Italian and Mexican descent, who make up the majority of those of non-African ancestry in the area.

The Near West Side is a world of the young and undereducated. More than 40 per cent of all the people living on the Near West Side are under eighteen, while fewer than 6 per cent are over sixty-five. The median number of school years completed is slightly more than eight—the end of junior high school.

Poverty is endemic on the West Side—in relation to the level of material life common to most residents of Chicago. The median annual family income in the area is about $4,000, compared with nearly $7,000 for the city as a whole.

1. The facts reported in the next six paragraphs come from Evelyn M. Kitagawa and Karl E. Taeuber, eds., *Local Community Fact Book: Chicago Metropolitan Area 1960* (Chicago Community Inventory, University of Chicago, 1963), pp. 2, 3, 70, 71, 216, 220, 326, 329, 331, 333.

The percentage of families having less than $3,000 per year is about 38, compared to about 14 for the city as a whole; those having more than $10,000 per year are only about 5 per cent, compared with more than 20 per cent for the entire city.

Housing conditions are a further dimension of the poverty of the Near West Side: about 45 per cent of the housing units in the area are substandard, compared to only about 15 per cent for the city as a whole. The median value of units occupied by their owners is only about $12,000, compared with about $18,000 for the city. More than 25 per cent of all housing units have more than one person per room, while the figure for the entire city is only about 12 per cent.

The proportions of individuals on government assistance are still another dimension of the poverty in the area. Approximately 25 per cent of all persons living in the area are on public assistance (welfare), while only about 8 per cent of the entire population of Chicago receives this kind of help. And while about 3.3 per cent of the work force of the Near West Side receives unemployment compensation, only 1.7 per cent of the Chicago work force does so. Only about 5 per cent of the Chicago work force is unemployed, in contrast to nearly 12 per cent of the Near West Side work force.

The Near West Side has one of the highest rates of alcoholism of any area in the city and a disproportionate share of the city's juvenile delinquents.

All of these figures include the islands of more affluent white people who live in the area. The extent of unpleasant living conditions and less than subsistence incomes among blacks in the area is much higher than the comparable figures for whites. Blacks are much worse off than is indicated by these figures. Indeed, their condition of material life can accurately be described as medieval.

The Near West Side is among the oldest of the many communities that comprise metropolitan Chicago. The town of Chicago was incorporated in 1835, and much of what is now the Near West Side was included in the expanding bounds of the city by 1851. In the early years of Chicago history there was much industrial and railroad activity on the Near West Side. Many major American railroads constructed tracks, yards, and terminals in the area. In the 1840's lumber companies, foundries, sash and door mills, and flour mills constructed facilities. The 1850's witnessed the addition of more foundries and the construction of planing mills, grain elevators, and what was for many years the city's largest stock yard.

The industrial boom was accompanied by rapid increases in population, especially in the 1850's; the population doubled between 1853 and 1856. The new demand for housing was met by the construction of many small frame cottages. The main nationalities represented in these early years on the Near West Side were German, Irish, and Scandanavian. The population doubled again during the decade of the 1860's, and pushed up even more rapidly after 1871, the year of the great Chicago fire. The fire did little damage to the West Side, and as a result, many who were burned out elsewhere sought new residences there. By the turn of the century many of the old inhabitants of the area, especially the Irish and Germans, had moved further west to more attractive locations. They were replaced by more recent immigrants—Italians, Poles, Russians (predominantly Jews), and Greeks. This new wave of humanity was accompanied by a new wave of industrial activity—new warehouses, wholesale houses, and manufacturing plants.

The peak population of the area—more than 200,000 people—was reached in about 1920; and it has declined steadily since then. The only exception to this even decline was during the 1940's, with a large increase in the black population of the area. Black people had been moving into the Near West Side since World War I, but their numbers did not become appreciable until World War II. The black fraction of the Near West Side population increased from 17 per cent in 1930 to more than 50 per cent in 1960.

The Near West Side began its history with the history of the City of Chicago. Its maiden years were boom years, full of population growth and economic expansion. It experienced the successive waves of change in ethnic composition familiar in the chronologies of many American cities. Since 1920 its population has fallen off, though its industrial activity has remained lively. Now a relatively large proportion of the land on the Near West Side is devoted to industry. Exclusive of the huge medical center complex and the campus of the University of Illinois at Chicago Circle, the nonindustrial land that is not vacant is occupied by multiple-family dwellings. Only about one out of ten of the housing units in these structures was built since 1940, and almost all of the residential structures built since the 1920's are public housing projects.

The usual expressways and urban renewal projects that have come to lower class American urban areas are also part of the present configuration of the Near West Side. Though these projects have removed many dilapidated structures from the Near West Side, they have not substantially contributed to the renovation of the area in a way that would improve the nature of material life and the physical environment of those who live in it.

The Near West Side is an ugly and stagnant place. It is physically unattractive. Its people are poor and unhappy. Efforts to improve it have been largely ineffective.

The majority of the residents of the Near West Side are poor and black. That is clear from the numbers used to describe the conditions of life there. But the numbers obscure how human beings deal with one another in any circumstance, and this is especially true of those used to describe the Near West Side. Many writers have attempted to describe the ways of life of poor black people in urban America.[2] One informative description is Charles Keil's; he writes in *Urban Blues*:

The unique and full status of Negro culture is only partly dependent on the basic institutional elements, such as Church and family, that do not fit white American specifications. On another and perhaps more fundamental level, the shared sensibilities and common understandings of the Negro ghetto, its modes of perception and expression, its channels of communication, are predominantly auditory and tactile rather than

2. For example, see Claude Brown, *Manchild in the Promised Land* (Macmillan, 1965); Horace R. Cayton and St. Clair Drake, *Black Metropolis* (Harper and Row, 1962); Kenneth B. Clark, *Dark Ghetto* (Harper and Row, 1965). Earlier writings describing black life and culture in America are analyzed in Harold Cruse's excellent volume, *The Crisis of the Negro Intellectual* (William Morrow, 1967).

visual and literate. Sensibilities are of course matters of degree, and the sense ration or "rationality" of a particular culture can't be measured precisely. Nevertheless, the prominence of aural perception, oral expression, and kinesic codes or body movement in Negro life—its sound and feel—sharply demarcate the culture from the irrational white world outside the ghetto. Negro and white Americans share the same general language (superficially a good argument for those who would relegate the Negro to a subcultural corner in homogenized America), but their attitudes toward that language are polarized. In white America, the printed word—the literary tradition—and its attendant values, are revered. In the Negro community, more power resides in the spoken word and oral tradition— good talkers abound and the best gain power and prestige, but good writers are scarce. It is no accident that much of America's slang is provided by Negro culture. Nor is it strange that Negro music and dance have become America's music and dance.

What I have found initially mysterious, however, is the almost universal disregard for the cultural framework that has fostered these forms of expression. Writers, including writers on Negro life, have a vested interest in literacy and the visual world view, to be sure, and some may simply be deaf to the pervasive aural-oral qualities of Negro culture. Then too, real rhetoric and ritual, the pattern and form, heart and soul of Negro expression, are largely unknown in white America. Indeed, the words themselves have taken on decidedly negative connotations—rhetoric: bombastic oratory, trickery, meaningless word play; ritual: dry formality, perfunctory action, unthinking and meaningless behavior. In the literary or typographic world, the labels mere rhetoric and ritualistic are the kiss of death. From this perspective, Negro culture heroes must appear as entertainers at best or at worst as clowns. Finally, a substantial number of influential Americans (poli-

ticians, white liberals, the Negro middle class) see Negro
culture as a threat if they can see it at all.[3]

Black people are in some ways different from white people in the American setting. It is difficult for most of us
who live in the cultures of affluent America to see this. For
the blacks we see first hand are, in their posture of the
newly arrived, likely to be the most avid defenders of and
participants in middle class ways: they are very much like
white people, perhaps more like white people than are
whites themselves. What we fail to see is the black man
who is most common in urban America—the man who lives
in a world of *sound* that is different from the world of *sight*
that others inhabit. The black man's way of looking at
things and his very style of life—closely bound together—
are different from those of others. His speech is more mel-
lifluous and expressive. His gestures are smoother and
freer. His emotions are more frequently—with some important exceptions described later on—exhibited without shame,
instead of bound up in some inner ulceration. His understanding and intelligence are somewhat different. To an
extent, his social reality is not the same.

The social tableau of life in the black community—and of
urban life in particular—is painted from a different palette
than that of the affluent classes, black or white. This may
be seen every instant in the neighborhoods of the poor and
black in the ways people deal with one another. But it is
most forcefully brought to an outsider in the well-attended
evening sessions at successful, lower class bars and night
clubs.

3. Charles Keil, *Urban Blues* (University of Chicago, 1966), pp.
16–18.

Most of us know what an evening in middle class white "cocktail lounges" is like. The bar is dark and comfortably appointed. The waiters and other attendants are soft-spoken and efficient. Frequently there is music—which may be a string orchestra, some bastardized Latin American melody, or the upsetting and jerky sound of bad white "rock." Any evening crowd is likely to feature pairs of men talking over their straight or crooked business, pairs of young men and women come to discover one another, pairs of old men and women come collectively to escape one another, an occasional prostitute or quiet hustler, perhaps a homosexual or two, and that face—always that face: the big one reddened by a hundred broken blood vessels and fronted by a bulbous nose grained from too much drink. Few people will make friends. There will be no fights. Almost everyone will pay his own bill.

What happens in lower class black bars is quite something else. There is *always* music—and not the background noise that passes for music in white bars—but the bold and gripping sound of the blues, coming usually from a juke box. It is always turned up very, very loud—so loud that the whole room becomes an extension of the machine. Indeed, when you walk into such a bar when there is a good crowd, you are not so much stepping into a bar with a juke box as into a music machine that happens incidentally to contain a bar and people. The room is the instrument, and those who are in it for the moment are not individuals but part of the music.

Frequently there is dancing: not the fox-trot or samba, not even the jerky motions of the now stylish discotheque dancing—but the smooth and beautiful gestures that glorify the blues, rather than mock it, unlike many of the dances of the young and white in America. There is always talk and laughter, and many transactions of business. People are bought and sold, reputations are won and lost, but new friends are made and old friendships are reaffirmed. And amid all the noise and commotion, the music and smoke, the deadening effects of alcohol, or the expanding effects of a recent taste of marijuana—amid all of this the blues emerges dominant; the blues runs the talk and noise, clears away the ugliness and violence of life, causes us to be able to stand all that. And in the bosom of such a scene one may witness the most moving celebration of humanity to be found in America.

It is a celebration that says in a very straightforward way: he tried to kill us all, one way or another, or to cause us to kill one another; he *does* kill many of us, and many of us *do* perish at the hands of our brothers. Yet we live—and we are men. This is no last ditch concentration-camp escapism; rather it is the time-worn assertion of a social self that is both critic and competitor of the mainstream American social self. It is the celebration of an alternative to the mainstream way of life—to the mainstream world view.

Capsule History

Like the way of life on the West Side, the history of the West Side Organization is not central to this work. Yet it is important in placing WSO in perspective.

Any brief chronology of the life of even a single human being is likely to contain minor inaccuracies and plain distortions, for it is impossible to reduce human experience in the disciplines of verbal expression to themes and histories portraying the rich detail of daily life. Such reductions of the experiences of groups of human beings related to one another in social organization are even more questionable. While it is clear that much is omitted from the following brief organizational history, the few events around which it is structured have been selected to sketch the developments from which the story of the organization's leaders is extracted.

INITIAL ATTEMPTS AT MOBILIZATION

The first steps taken to mobilize potential leaders in Chicago's Near West Side ghetto were exploratory, and their results were mixed. In July 1964 five clergymen and theological students were sent by the Urban Training Center, the Chicago City Missionary Society, and the Meadville Theological Seminary to work on the development of an indigenous community organization on the Near West Side. The first move the group made was to seek out and to engage chronically unemployed men in the neighborhood. Originally it was thought that this would be a simple matter, involving tours of local pool rooms, bars, and street corners, where the unemployed could be found and interviewed. But the social distance between outsiders and members of the community was so great, the suspicion of the people of the Near West Side so strong, that direct approaches failed.

In the wake of this failure, the group tried to secure help from well-established organizations in the community—the usual churches and labor unions. With the counsel of these agencies, they formulated a list of unemployed men and sent out more than two hundred fifty personal letters inviting them to an open meeting for the discussion of conditions in the area.

Four people showed up for the meeting—yet another failure. But the clergymen and community residents who had come sat and talked informally about many things— especially about explanations for the meager turnout. And again, there seemed to be a barrier separating the clergymen from a deep understanding of the West Side community and the mental cast of its people. There was a strong implication in the conversation that invitations to such meetings were regarded by neighborhood residents as an affront—as on effort by outsiders to "mess with them."

To pierce these barriers, in an act of significant personal commitment, eight of the men at the meeting—four from the community and four clergymen—decided to live together for a week on a one-to-one basis in the homes of the four community residents in the hope that the outsiders could gain a better understanding of West Side life. Considerable progress was made during this week in increasing the understanding of the outsiders and in consolidating the personal commitment made by all eight. But even so, both insiders and outsiders had a long road to travel before any fundamental understanding, empathy, and trust was to develop. Richard Wright's reflections in his brutal novel *Native Son* are closer to the truth about relations between whites and blacks in America than many people realize. There is a certain intimacy that can be achieved easily, but efforts such as those made by these eight men are forever clouded by the legacy of racial hatred and suspicion left us by our predecessors. These men did not become "soul brothers" in a week; they had only become familiar enough with one another to be a little less afraid of going on together to seek new relationships.

At the end of this week all were discouraged by the lack of response of citizens of the community to the first over-tures, but concurrently, all were encouraged by the sense of personal commitment to each other in the brief time together.

FURTHER EFFORTS

Building on this commitment, the small group canvassed their friends in the neighborhood in efforts to persuade more people to join in further meetings. The size of the group gradually increased as a growing interest in the nascent organization developed. The feelings of optimism were so well advanced in the small group by the fall of 1964 that they felt ready to secure office space and furnishings. Fi-nanced by a grant of several thousand dollars from the Urban Training Center, they soon found that having an office helped immensely in recruiting additional members. In addition to the Reverend Robert Strom, the Reverend Donald Keating, and several other clergymen, four men from the neighborhood were employed as full-time workers. One of these, Chester Robinson, was to become the execu-tive director of the organization later. Several men who had participated in the very first meetings stayed on as volunteer and paid workers; among them was John Crawford, now a full-time staff member and a key figure in the organization. At this early stage of development these black men from the community could not really be called leaders of the organization because there was no organization to be led, and because they had not yet the full confidence—which was to come later—that the clergymen involved were really not neocolonialists, men come to exploit them under the pretense of helping them. Many of their friends in the community repeatedly asked them why they were "letting those white guys front them." They were caught in a vise: on one side their old friends who were black suspected them of selling out to the white clergymen, while on the other, they were encouraged by the commitment they felt the clergymen had made to them. The tensions were not only social, manifest in the pressures from both sides, but also psychological, manifest in deep feelings of confusion within several of the early participants in the organization. The resolution of these social and personal tensions is the genius of the West Side Organization, the very startling consolidation of a small group of black men (with some whites) in a common cause and the consolidation of the personalities of many of the participants in WSO.

GROWTH

Building on the increasing commitment of the growing body of participants in WSO, the organization began to take shape and to develop a program out of needs that its members perceived as the needs of the Near West Side.

In many of the early meetings possibilities for organizational programs had been discussed, but very little progress was made until a dramatic confrontation between WSO and a local laundry brought the organization to the attention of many people in the community. Until this confrontation, though people on the Near West Side had heard about the organization, only the few who had been reached directly by WSO staff members had any real notion what it was like. When it was learned that the Centennial Laundry, located in the heart of the Near West Side black community, as a matter of explicit policy would not hire blacks in other than menial jobs, WSO demanded that the policy be changed. After a series of pickets and negotiations, the laundry acquiesced and agreed to change its policies, interviewing black applicants for all available jobs in consultation with WSO. The change in policy was not significant in itself, but the by-products were crucial to the early development of WSO as a force in its community. It became known as a tough-minded, militant organization able to get results. And following the Centennial Laundry conflict, many more people began to come into WSO to seek help with their problems.

Most of the programs of the organization have emerged from what staff members thought were recurrent and important requests for help from local residents. The major programs have included employment counseling, servicing welfare grievances, publication of the neighborhood newspaper *West Side Torch*, informal remedial education for adults and adolescents, and social protest action. All of the programs have been successful with the exception of the educational program, which was dropped because of insufficient teaching manpower and inadequate classroom facilities. The summed achievements are remarkable: more than a thousand jobs (none at less than $3,000 a year) in the first two years, more than a thousand welfare grievances handled (all with results satisfactory to the welfare recipients involved), a financially self-sufficient, free newspaper with a circulation of more than 10,000, and a reputation

among other black organizations for being an able participant in the street marches and demonstrations thematic in
expressions of social protest in contemporary America.

Of all the programs, the Welfare Union is the most vigorous and important. WSO did not intend originally to work
on welfare grievances on a large scale. But in the fall of
1964 a woman came to WSO with a problem. She had
heard of the organization, and though she did not really
know what it was, she felt her problem would be treated
with sympathy. She was on public assistance (welfare),
and one of her children, a girl of fifteen, had chronic leu-
kemia. Treatments for the disease had run up a debt of
several thousand dollars, which the Cook County Department of Public Aid refused to pay when they learned that
the girl was pregnant. After about six weeks of intermittent
negotiations, WSO secured full payment of the bills from
the authorities. The organization had dealt with a few other
such welfare grievances previously, but this was a much
more important case than any of the others, and the victory
was significant.

As others in the community on public assistance learned
of this success, they began to come to WSO for help with
their problems with welfare officials. Seizing on this new
traffic, WSO developed a Welfare Union which now services
the grievances of welfare recipients, working out of offices
in many other parts of the city as well as on the Near West
Side.

All the programs have grown slowly from the inception
of the organization. There have been fluctuations in the
levels of activity in all programs, but the pattern of growth
has largely been an even increase. There have been many
changes in the organization in its brief history: volunteer

staff members have come and gone; a variety of relationships with the civil rights movement have come and gone;
new leaders have emerged. But looking back on its brief
history, no large change has taken place in the orientation
of the organization since the opening months of its life.
This crucial period when the major participants in WSO
committed themselves to the work of the organization was
by far the most significant time in the chronology of WSO's
evolution.

INSURRECTION

In July 1966 there was an insurrection of Chicago's West
Side.[4] No one can fully discuss the West Side Organization
without dealing with it, even though its occurrence should
not surprise anyone, and even though it is peripheral to
the major themes of the essay.

July 12, 1966, was an extremely hot and uncomfortable
day for most residents of Chicago. It was the crest of an
extended heat wave; tempers were short; nerves were worn;
people were edgy. There were few channels of relief for
the people of the West Side from these intense and abundant
discontents. It was possible to go to a distant public swim-
ming pool, and having waited a long time, to secure the
questionable relief of a brief swim in a jammed pool. It
was possible to sit on a folding chair on the sidewalk in the
shade of buildings. It was possible to go to a movie. But
all these were inadequate; at best providing only symbolic
relief from the summer's intense heat.

4. The description of WSO's role in the riot is taken from an un-
published paper by Rev. Bernard O. Brown entitled "WSO and the
Riot on the Near West Side."

Turning to another such symbolic relief, a few residents of the West Side had turned on a fire hydrant on Roosevelt Road, only a few blocks from WSO headquarters. Though it is against the law, fire hydrants are customarily opened on very hot days in many poor neighborhoods in American cities, Chicago among them. But on this day the police insisted on closing the hydrant, even though they had apparently allowed others in nearby neighborhoods to remain open. Several teenagers demanded that the hydrant be turned on—and proceeded to turn it back on themselves.

In the confusion following this initial defiance of the police, the hydrant was turned on and off several times, and the altercation between one or two policemen and a handful of black teenagers grew over several hours into a period of violent insurrection that lasted for several days, ultimately involving the occupation of the West Side by the forces of the National Guard.

WSO acted as an agent of pacification and as a communications center for various participants in the insurrection, from members of teenage gangs to the police. WSO leaders went out into the crowd and told people to go home, to get off the street. The WSO main office served as a meeting place for concerned community residents and as a haven for white people trapped in the area. If a single word may be used to characterize the activities of WSO during the madness and violence of the insurrection, it is heroism, for the organization's leaders took grave risks to their personal safety in trying to stop the disturbance.

The riot was remarkable in many ways, mostly in being so limited and restrained. There was much less violence than there could have been. Certainly many people were injured, including a young black girl killed by a "stray" bullet. But no policemen were killed, and though many stores were robbed and burned, no single building was demolished. The riot was a mild disturbance indeed. Further, there was no substantial organization in the outburst. Small cliques of individuals were seen looting or preparing Molotov cocktails together, but even these were few in number and loosely organized.

Some accounts of the riot appearing in the presentations of the news media described WSO as a band of violent revolutionaries who, they claimed, were the instigators and organizers of the riot.[5] But no evidence was ever presented to substantiate these charges, and in fact WSO played no such role.

Many in Chicago had questioned WSO's position on the use of violence before the riot. But the riot pressed WSO into the position of having to show its colors in plain view for everyone to see. And those colors were—for the time being—those of an opponent of violence, whether by the police and soldiers or by members of the black community. The organization could easily have promoted and sustained the riot, increasing its intensity and extending its duration, yet it did just the opposite in seeking to limit both. This single set of events is the most compelling refutation that can be offered to those who claim the organization is presently violent and destructive in its posture toward social action.

AFTER THE INSURRECTION

Many people in the city and in the Near West Side community received this message clearly. During the half-year

5. For example, see the New York *Post*, July 20, 1966, p. 1.

following the riot the police, local businessmen, the nearby branch of the University of Illinois, and several public and private welfare agencies went to WSO for guidance in dealing with the people of the Near West Side, and they formed independent organizations to promote the improvement of the community—that is, to ward off further disturbances. Many of the institutions and persons had expressed little or no concern for the community and its welfare before the riot. And even though their efforts have so far made little substantive difference in the nature of life on the West Side, the fact that they have embarked on symbolic gestures of community concern is encouraging. I hope that their concern will engage the real and lasting problems of the Near West Side in a more responsible way before it is too late.

HOPES FOR THE FUTURE

The underlying spirit of these new efforts is negative. They are attempts to alter the community just enough so that the investments of outsiders will not be jeopardized. Many West Siders who follow local political developments closely see such efforts as an affront, believing that they are programs to change merely the color of the walls of the concentration camp in the hope that the inmates will think less of tearing them down. What is required are programs to promote control of the community over its productive energies and to improve the mode of material existence, while maintaining its cultural harmonies. And unless some substantial progress is made in accomplishing these changes, there will probably be a major insurrection soon, rather than continued brief skirmishes like that of 1966.

Executives of the institutions in the community can make

a substantial contribution to the required alterations in the community. But without the vigorous participation of community residents in new programs, little progress will be made no matter how generous institutions are with their resources.[6] The West Side Organization provides a nucleus of leadership and an image that can facilitate the transformation of the West Side and its people—the transformation necessary to avoid violent revolutionary upheaval, but more important, the transformation necessary for the black people of this slice of America to become full participants in American life on their own terms, terms that preserve their culture and social identity, and that guarantee them some control over their community life and destiny.

To accomplish this the West Side Organization needs to find some way of increasing its budget. For the duration of its existence it has been underfinanced in spite of the generosity of its supporters. Only about half of the present full-time staff receive any salary at all, and the few salaries that are paid (ranging fro $75 to $100 a week) are inadequate. The office space is inadequate—a dilapidated one-room store front. The transportation facilities are inadequate. And the organization's finances are inadequate in all other categories. It is difficult for WSO to manage the work it is presently engaged in; and the expansion required to promote the transformation of the West Side and its people is impossible within the constraints of the present budget.

6. This point is made clearly in a *New Republic* editorial (June 24, 1967, p. 8): "Maximum feasible participation is the central . . . core of the poverty program. Personal dignity and the knowledge that one can do something to improve his own life are in the long run more important than a few hydrants turned on in June and the frightened gestures Washington makes toward the ghetto, when, as it does in the summertime, violence seems imminent."

The required additional financing could come from a number of sources: local merchants, private foundations, revenues from WSO-created community business enterprises, or some local or national public agency, such as the Office of Economic Opportunity. The real possibilities of securing additional funding are not easy to assess. At the moment it is not clear what the future of WSO will be, though it is clear what it has to be in order to promote the development of the Near West Side.

Some of the Men Who Made WSO

The work that led to the establishment of the West Side Organization was initiated by people from outside the community. The beginning efforts were conceived, financed, and carried out by Protestant clergymen. Certainly there were many people involved in these activities, but the three prime movers were the Reverends Archie Hargraves, Donald Benedict, and Robert Strom.

ARCHIE HARGRAVES

To the extent that WSO was conceived by any single individual, it was conceived by Archie Hargraves. His long experience working with impoverished black people in American cities led him to advocate a number of unusual guidelines for community organization—the guidelines used to mold the West Side Organization. Briefly, they rest on the notion that oppression relegates men and women of great talent to low positions in the web of American social hierarchies. Those who would seek to alleviate oppression in America should try to mobilize these men and women to direct their talents and energies to resisting oppression, rather than to the pursuits of gaming, swindling, and trafficking in their fellows. These assertions are diametrically opposed to the abundantly argued thesis that only individuals with adequate formal education—middle class people —have the skills requisite for providing political leadership for the poor and black in the effort to break the cyclical perpetuation of their oppression.[7]

The education and experience that brought Hargraves to propound these guidelines is an unusual combination of theological and social science studies, of working in slums and in church bureaucracies. Born in North Carolina early in the second decade of this century, and raised by his grandmother, he excelled in his secondary school and college studies. His college years were spent at North Carolina Agricultural and Technical College, a state-supported Negro school; and since the Depression limited his financial means, his progress was interrupted by periods of work—as a laborer and newspaper reporter, and in various other jobs. Following college, he went on to Union Theological Seminary in New York City, where he earned a Bachelor of Divinity degree and acquired an interest in social science.

It was during these years in New York that he began his career as a community organizer, working in Harlem as one of the founders of the East Harlem Parish. When he had completed his ministerial training, he continued to work with the poor in Harlem and entered a religion, arts, and sciences program conducted jointly by Union Theological Seminary

7. Many have made this argument. See especially Crane Brinton's *The Anatomy of Revolution*, revised and expanded edition (Random House, 1965), pp. 101–105.

and Columbia University. After three years of study in the intellectual intersections of religion with literature, social science, and philosophy, he had completed all of the work required for a doctoral degree with the exception of a dissertation. He is among the most broadly educated of American clergymen.

Terminating his studies and his work with the East Harlem Parish, he was sent to Chicago by his church, the United Church of Christ (then Congregational), to establish an organization like the East Harlem Parish on the West Side of that city. He succeeded in doing so in the years between 1951 and 1956. Continuing his work in lower class black communities, Hargraves was pastor of the Nazarene Congregational Church in Brooklyn, New York, from 1956 to 1961, where he started many community programs to encourage adolescents to stay in school and to promote the employment of young blacks in local industries; he also conducted protest demonstrations at a Brooklyn medical school (financed by the State of New York) against its discriminatory hiring policies. From 1961 to 1964 he was a church executive, Secretary of the Urban Church Department of the United Church of Christ. Following this duty, he took his present job as Director of Mission Development of the Urban Training Center in Chicago, an organization financed by national church organizations and foundations, whose purpose is to train ministers for careers in the hearts of American cities.

This splendid career of community organization, social science training, teaching, and administration brought Hargraves to Chicago in 1964—fully equipped with the skills, contacts, and other resources necessary to initiate an organizational effort like WSO, and fully determined to do it.

ROBERT STROM

At 35 Reverend Robert Strom is younger than Hargraves, and his experience, though it shares some themes with that of Hargraves, is different.

Strom, a white man, was born in Elyria, Ohio, a small industrial town in the north central part of that state. He was raised and schooled in Elyria, and worked his way through Oberlin College on a job in a steel mill. He went on to Princeton Theological Seminary, where he earned a Bachelor of Divinity degree; then was ordained a Presbyterian minister.

In contrast to the experience of Hargraves, Strom's first two posts were in churches in Bergen County, New Jersey, very near New York. His views of the functions of clergymen and churches in society, even then built around constructive social criticism, were at odds with those of his parishioners, causing great tensions in his work.

At this critical juncture, the experience of Hargraves, a black man from the South and an expert in organizing the black poor in urban America, and the experience of Strom, a white man schooled in small towns and suburbs, but enchanted with urban life, merged, and Strom was offered a job working with Hargraves in metropolitan Chicago. After a time this job developed into a full-time endeavor at building the West Side Organization. If Hargraves is the fountainhead of ideas and theory that set the style of the initial efforts at developing WSO, Strom is the key implementer and working critic of these theories and ideas. It was he who went into the West Side, engaged its people, and encouraged them to work with him in making WSO. Again, several others were involved, but Strom is the most important.

DONALD BENEDICT

Reverend Donald Benedict is the executive director of the Chicago City Missionary Society,[8] an interdenominational organization greatly concerned with ameliorating the great problems of the city and at the same time linked through its board of directors to the centers of power and influence in Chicago politics. Where Hargraves and Strom have conceived and founded WSO, Benedict provided most of the financial resources necessary for the work.

Many of the major social institutions in America would balk at supporting the proposition that the poor and black are capable of acting and speaking on their own behalf. And under most circumstances, even American religious organizations would not support this view. But the peculiar combination of people and interest, and the presence of a relatively strong and independent interdenominational organization like the Chicago City Missionary Society, produced a unique set of circumstances enabling some clergymen to put skill, money, and time into propounding this view in the form of the initiation of the West Side Organization. Though Benedict's style is essentially different from that of Hargraves and Strom—he is chiefly an administrator, they are skilled organizers of the poor—he has provided substantial financial support for WSO from the coffers of his organization.

8. The name of this organization has recently been changed to the Community Renewal Society. But since it was called by its former name during the full period of the research for this volume, it is referred to by that name throughout the pages that follow.

THE BLACK PEOPLE OF THE NEAR WEST SIDE

Hargraves, Strom, and Benedict provided ideas, organizing skills, and financial resources necessary to begin WSO. But the major part of the work—the work that has made WSO a going concern—has been done by the people of the West Side themselves, especially by the leaders and other major participants in the organization. By many measures, the work that Hargraves, Strom, Benedict, and other outsiders put into the organization was huge. But in its totality this work was but the first and most meager of a long chain of events leading to the present state of development of WSO. Without the skills, dedication, and sacrifice of the people of the Near West Side, the effort would certainly have failed.

Though the time and energy and willingness to make sacrifices brought to the organization by its black leaders have been of great importance, perhaps the major contribution of these men is the application of their own very strong personalities (perhaps even the *redirection* of their personalities) and their knowledge of life on the Near West Side to work they thought was important.

Life on the West Side is different from life in other parts of American society. And it is not only different in wealth, but also in culture. People who inhabit the West Side are not simply poor Americans, who may be viewed as deficient aspirants to the affluent American ways of life. Rather, their ways of looking at the social world, their ways of treating one another, the very nature of their knowledge and intelligence, are not the same as those of the America portrayed in the mass media. Only a man who has been raised in that way of life, who has been socialized to its norms, and who at the same time has the intelligence and sensitivity to be able to communicate to both ways of life—the mainstream and that of the West Side—only this kind of man can adequately mobilize and lead the poor and black in contemporary urban America.

Strom and Hargraves are intelligent and sensitive men who have a profound understanding of life on the West Side, yet because they have not internalized its norms, because they are not full participants in its culture, their abilities to communicate with people on the West Side are limited—much more limited than are those of the indigenous leaders. Without the skills and understanding that these men have brought to the organization, it would have failed to reach the people on the West Side who have not been reached by any other agency of change—most of the people.

5

ACTIVITIES AND STRUCTURE
OF WSO

Between 1964 and the present, the West Side Organization evolved into a vigorous enterprise. But it is difficult in a report of this kind to chronicle all the events of organizational development to the moment in the style of the journalist. The following summary is a report of the state of the organization and its work as of August 1966.

Activities

WSO has more work than it can possibly do. The demands that the community of poor black people in Chicago has made on staff members for help in finding employment, for representation to the welfare authorities, and for education and information daily overload the interactional circuits linking paid and volunteer participants in the web of WSO organization. And these activities, the main business of WSO, do not include the work involved in conducting community meetings and in meeting with other leaders of black freedom movements to build and break coalitions and to haggle over policy.

The various activities of the organization are not conducted by well-defined subunits as in a factory or insurance company. Though the major activities are separable in the mind of the WSO clientele as they view the organization, participation of single individuals in many activities blurs the organizational structure and binds all of the major activities together in a subtle but cohesive way.

EMPLOYMENT

One of the central concerns of the organization in the beginning was unemployment. In its early phases of activity, the organization was thought of as something that would be created out of the problems of unemployed men on the Near West Side. The difficulties of finding and keeping jobs were, therefore, central in the initial discussion of organizational prospects for action.

But unemployment among the poor and black is not simply a matter of finding and keeping jobs. Properly understood, it is a way of life. Frequently, self-appointed oracles of the public mind from newspapers and magazines, and officially designated ones from various government agencies nearby in Washington, point to the problem of black unemployment as one of insufficient skills.[1] Black people, they

1. For a description of some of the programs based on this view, see Sar A. Levitan, "Programs in Aid of the Poor," in *Hearings before the Subcommittee on Executive Reorganization of the Committee on Gov-*

say, do not know what is necessary to man the sophisticated machines and to cope with the complex organizational structures of modern—and not-so-modern—American corporations and governments. To a certain extent this statement is true, but it is an inadequate explanation of the fact that unemployment in many black ghettos is more than twice that in other parts of the cities of America.

Most analysts would have us believe that the lives and outlooks of all Americans of roughly equivalent economic statuses are about the same. Anyone who has the requisite skill, and appropriate physical and personality characteristics for a certain job can get such a job, and he will have the same kind of experience working on that job as anyone else. All a black man needs to do is to go to school and learn a trade. This sad distortion of the facts entirely ignores the human elements in the situation—in particular, the effects of oppression on America's black men and women. *Black people are oppressed men.* They are oppressed initially in the subtle psychological confrontations of child and society. Living in a society where prominent authority figures are white, and where black men are featured as incompetent and foolish, black children at an early age become aware that theirs is an inferior social status and do not develop the level of self-esteem that other children do. Their feelings of worthlessness are frequently nurtured and reinforced in their dealings with others: (1) inhumane treatment by public school teachers with responses warped by their inability to cope with the transition from the relatively tranquil life of middle class universities to what they perceive as the violence and instability of urban slums; (2) brutal treatment

ernment Operations, United States Senate, 89th Congress, 2nd session, Part 2, pp. 459–486.

by policemen with strange conceptions of the difference between order and disorder; and (3) cruelty by parents whose aggressive impulses toward a hostile world are often displaced on their offspring. Even as children many American blacks are not likely to hope for anything—achievement, wealth, happiness, or long life.

Adolescent experiences build upon this childhood foundation, and the feelings of hopelessness and self-hatred are more firmly and elaborately woven into the fabric of personality. Sometime early in adolescence most blacks begin to perceive from the experiences of friends and relatives that the rewards of education are not very great. They may hear that a good friend, who had become a machinist in the navy, was hired by a local firm only to be referred to as "boy" by the foreman, beaten by his coworkers after five o'clock, and given the worst machine to work at even after he had gained two years of seniority. They might hear that an older cousin who had graduated from high school was washing dishes in a local restaurant. They might hear that an uncle who was a high school teacher had been called "nigger" by his white principal repeatedly, had appealed to higher authorities in the school administration, and had resigned when he received no response. Such stories are characteristic of the information these children get about the world and their place in it. Many quit school, or become lethargic or violent if they stay, which is not surprising.

When they are confronted for the first time with the necessity of going to work, frequently at the age of ten or twelve, many are anxious to do so, for it offers a possibility of enhancing their independence and self-esteem. At this juncture there is a momentary flash of hope. But it usually passes so quickly that it leaves no memory, as they find that all of

the ugly stories they heard earlier were true and they become despondent, ultimately quitting or being fired for
insubordination. A great many, however, never experience
the dimmest glimmer of hope.

Then they are unemployed.

They lack the self-esteem that would allow them to
believe that they are competent and useful members of
society. And of those who manage to develop the requisite
self-image in spite of the oppression experienced in childhood and adolescence, many will not try to get ahead in
the normal ways because they are not willing to be abused
verbally and physically for a salary, when they could be
making much more money without it in criminal pursuits.

These men are everywhere in the West Side, and in similar
sections of all major cities in the United States. They can be
seen playing checkers or rolling dice in the street—or
drinking pints of wine from paper bags. A few can be seen
hustling the community for the criminal and political syndicates, or for themselves.

They are without hope of ordinary achievement, without
any single sign to sustain them in anything but their hatred
of the society that brutalizes their very souls. You can see
them greet one another heartily in the street, laughing and
talking about better days or an old friend. But their intimacy
is something that cannot be shared—or even deeply understood by those who do not also share their hopelessness and
their understanding and hatred of their white and black
oppressors.

Unemployment is the blues. And the blues is a way of
life, a way of life from which no amount of alcohol or
barbiturates, save the ultimate dose, can provide escape. To
understand it and design programs to end it on the basis

of any notion of skill gaps misses the point—the point that America's black peoples are oppressed in the American social system—or, if you prefer, by white people and "their Negroes."

The WSO approach to unemployment has not missed the point, for it recognizes unemployment as a way of life that results from oppression. The staff of WSO have shared this way of life and this oppression, and are therefore able to comprehend the hopelessness and low self-esteem of many who come to them for help in finding employment. And further, they are able to deal with the cunning that the oppressed man develops as his major means of survival. WSO staff members are able to tell much of the time when an applicant is really interested in securing a job and when he is not. They are able to talk straight to applicants about jobs and about themselves, something that public and private employment agencies cannot do. Those who have had experiences with such agencies come to WSO suspiciously, even though they have been told that WSO is not a "front for the white folks." They are wary because they have never encountered anyone who tried to help them in the ways WSO has tried to help; their experience is crowded with hostile, indifferent, or foolish people who profess to be in the business of helping them—social workers, teachers, policemen, clergymen, and others. They become less apprehensive of WSO as their knowledge of the organization increases.

The fact that the staff of WSO are people who know the style of life of the Near West Side black community breaches many barriers that most of the best-intentioned outsiders never know about. Here the unemployed man is confronted with a small group of men who have known starvation, degradation, violence, and despair, who know the full meaning of the American black man's blues. And this sharing gives them more confidence than would a thousand social workers or all the ill-spent funds of the national war on poverty. For they know that WSO is not working for "the man"—the white man, the enemy.

The employment program is conducted almost entirely by Chester Robinson, the executive director, from his desk at 1527 West Roosevelt Road. He and his assistants survey the urban area of Chicago and build up files of companies that have openings. When someone comes to the office in his quest for a job, WSO operates as an employment agency, referring candidates to openings for which they may be suited. Follow-up interviews and inquiries are made to determine the disposition of referrals, though short financial and manpower resources have hurt this phase of the work.

From the summer of 1964 to August 1966 WSO secured more than a thousand jobs for residents of the West Side, none of them below the $3,000 annual salary of the top of the poverty scale. If the entire amount that WSO spent during that time, approximately $50,000 had been devoted to this employment service (which it was not), the average price per job would be a bit less than $75—a remarkable achievement by any standard.

The major problem in this area is to get people who *need* jobs to be able to *stand* them—to be able to stand and fight the abuse heaped on any black man who works for a white man's organization, the abuse that few white people are sensitive enough to see. And this is what WSO has done. Many have come to the organization who would otherwise still be on the street; WSO has helped soften the personal distress of the blues, the bitterly painful way of life called unemployment, the way of life engendered by oppression.

WELFARE GRIEVANCES

Unemployment was the point of departure in WSO's activities. But unemployment is only part of the problem, and soon the organization became involved in other areas. Since a large proportion of the people who live on the West Side are on public assistance, the Cook County Department of Public Aid is the major government institution impinging on the lives of the West Side's people. Some of those who work for this agency are dedicated to the humane treatment of the poor people they serve, but many of them in their work are cruel or indifferent to the poor. A particular incident of such cruelty and indifference is called a "welfare grievance."

Though handling welfare grievances was not one of the categories pondered as a possible focus for WSO action in the early days of the group, it was inevitable that a program for people on welfare be initiated, for mistreatment by the Department of Public Aid is as much a part of the black man's oppression on the Near West Side as in unemployment. WSO has been in the business of handling welfare grievances since early fall 1964, almost since its beginning. The catalyst that stimulated the development of the now burgeoning program was a case brought to the organization at that time (described in the preceding chapter).

With the success achieved in this case as a part of the WSO record, others in the neighborhood heard about the new activity at WSO in welfare and came in with other complaints. The volume of welfare grievances mushroomed in the first two years of operation, and the organization now has a total of five "Welfare Union locals"—units that handle welfare grievances—in parts of the city with high concentrations of welfare recipients, in the South Side black community, as well as in the West. Some of the people who man them are volunteers, though the key personnel are paid workers from the West Side. The entire organizational apparatus is headquartered at the Roosevelt Road office. It is called the WSO Welfare Union and is headed by William Darden.

When someone comes to one of the locals for help, the facts of his complaint are taken down on forms by a WSO worker, and if possible the matter is handled by a telephone call to the local welfare office. If this does not work, and if the complainant desires, the WSO official will accompany him to the local welfare office and plead his case to the welfare functionary who is causing the alleged problem. All WSO Welfare Union workers have a firm mastery of the relevant welfare laws and the independence to recognize when city officials are violating them, which happens frequently.[2] These skills have been mastered not through formal training but from daily work in the organization.

During its first two years, the Welfare Union handled more than a thousand grievances—all of them successfully. That is, they have handled only complaints that were justi-

2. This is not to say that all welfare caseworkers and their supervisors willfully violate the law all the time; most of them do not consistently and willfully violate the law in their mistreatment of welfare recipients. But there are a great many who do because they are poorly trained for their jobs. The result—mistreatment of recipients—is the same in either case.

fied, in which city officials were breaking administrative
policy or public law, and have secured a redress of the
grievances from the responsible officials. The initial grievance took more than six weeks to process; now no complaint
requires more than a single day.

There have been almost continual negotiations between
the WSO Welfare Union and other organizations created in
its image on the possibility of founding a citywide, or even
nationwide, union of welfare recipients. What the outcome
of these haggling sessions will be is unclear, but it is certain
that the WSO Welfare Union will not compromise its independence or effectiveness for the sake of such an affiliation.

It is hard for many to comprehend the basic inhumanity
of many officials of the welfare works in Chicago. It is hard
for them to believe that these people, whom most of us
have come to regard as "do-gooders" on a mission to help
the underprivileged, frequently treat welfare recipients as
if they were animals. They may conduct unannounced close
searches of recipients' homes. They may withhold recipients'
checks for no apparent reason. They may secure employment
for mothers of fatherless families of more than a half-dozen
children in the name of raising the mother's self-esteem,
while the actual result may be to reduce the family's income
and to leave the children uncared for. Some may even curse
black recipients and call them "niggers" without apparent
provocation.

Like unemployment, being on welfare is a way of life—a
way of life that no one, including residents of the West
Side, would live without compulsion. Certainly there are a
few people in Chicago for whom being on assistance is a
boon, but the amount of assistance and the way it is ad-
ministered are such that nearly everyone who must live this

way is unhappy about it—if not in a mood to participate in violent revolutionary action.

What WSO has done is to give welfare recipients a new perspective on their condition. It has shown them that even though they are unable to support themselves, they are still human beings and should have the right to be treated with dignity, not as they frequently are at the hands of welfare officials.

WSO is not in business to get as many people on the welfare dole as possible, as is frequently alleged. To the contrary, it is in business to get people *off* welfare through its efforts to reduce unemployment. The function of the Welfare Union is to insure that those who must remain on welfare get treated in accordance with law, administrative decree, and what it sees as the fundamental principles of human decency.

In the relations of West Side slum-dwellers to the white world, WSO is concerned as much with the nature of interpersonal relations as it is with goods and gold. A welfare grievance hurts, for it means that a family is temporarily without food, clothing, or carfare to get the children to school, but it is viewed as merely another manifestation of the contempt with which the white world, here represented by the white or middle class Negro welfare official, regards impoverished members of the black community.

EDUCATION

The education program has been hurt most by WSO's lack of adequate funding. In 1965 a large evening tutoring program for school children, literacy classes for adults, and typing classes for all ages started, and they even flourished for a time. The three programs were run in the evenings, manned by middle-class people from other parts of town. The typing program had to be discontinued because the noise from the machines impeded the function of the other programs, carried on at the same time in the single-roomed WSO headquarters, and because typewriters were difficult to secure and maintain. The other programs have continued, but at a lower level of activity than was originally projected.

The demand for these educational programs is great on the West Side, but WSO does not have the resources to service them all. WSO leaders have always encouraged residents of the community to take advantage of the training programs available through the United States Department of Labor, the Office of Economic Opportunity, and other government agencies. It is not the goal of WSO to be able to service all of the community's demands for education and training, but it does not even have the resources to do the kinds of things in this area that it can do better than any conceivable public authority—matters requiring the participant's confidence in the administering organization, such as the work in tutoring and adult literacy.

THE WEST SIDE *Torch*

The biweekly newspaper of WSO is a tabloid—like the New York *Daily News* or the Chicago *Sun-Times*—of eight to sixteen pages (and sometimes more). It is edited by Patricia Stock, a young white college graduate, and it has a small staff, including James Hallsell and Erskine Jones, both local residents, as managers of the financial and advertising parts of the business. Started originally as a handout news sheet in late 1965, it has grown to a respectable community newspaper financed by advertisements from local businessmen.

The *Torch* concentrates on community news and the most dramatic news of the Chicago and national freedom movement. It contains information about government services available to West Side citizens and carries editorials and a column for adolescents as more or less regular features.

The style of the *Torch* is exposé journalism, using blunt and emotion-charged prose to depict local problems, but it does not shade over into the inflammatory language and heavily biased reporting that characterize the journals and newspapers of political extremists of the right and left. It has carried pictures and reports that have seemed more sensationalist journalism than the reporting of facts—such as pictures of black people beaten by the police and pictures and reports of persons getting paid for their votes. But after all, life on the West Side *is* largely sensational—cruel, ugly, and often short. To report these events as the carefree, though plain, lives of weak, but happy, natives is not beneficial to anyone—on the West Side or anywhere else.

Its editorial policy is not laced with the ideology of any political party or movement, save generalized support for radical changes in the social position of black people in America.

For a long time the *Torch* was a marginal enterprise financially, but recently it has become self-supporting. And it is hoped that it will soon have enough paid subscribers and steady advertisers to become an even more successful, and perhaps even profitable, community venture.

OTHER ACTIVITIES

Jobs, schooling, welfare, a community newspaper—these are the major areas of WSO work, but there are other activities either carried on now or contemplated for the future.

First, the organization has always served as an informal communications and information center in the community. Many people come for information on such questions as how to get a doctor if you are broke, or how to get a discharge from the armed services reviewed. If residents of the community want information about how to deal with the outside world, they are likely to come to WSO—their buffer against the world. Second, a number of plans for expanding the activities of WSO have been discussed over its three-year history. There has been a recurrent suggestion that the organization start businesses in the community that would enhance WSO's financial independence and diminish the dependence of West Side residents on merchants in the community who charge too much and sell only shoddy merchandise. WSO would not become a holding company for these new enterprises, but it would organize group endeavors by West Siders in this direction with the hope that the successful new businesses would contribute to the financial support of WSO.

Formal and Informal Organization

Organization theory is among the oldest of human sciences. Dating from the Egyptian pyramid builders and the carefully designed bureaucracies of the early empires of the Far East, plain and obscure theories of how to organize human beings for the performance of various tasks form a rich and diverse literature. One distinction that has emerged is that between formal and informal organization. Formal organization is the pattern of authority and communication prescribed by those in a position to form or change an organization. Informal organization is the actual patterning of relations among participants in the organization as they go about their daily work. Formally, the legal assistant to the head of a large corporation may only advise his superior, while actually (or informally), he may not only render advice but also be an important executive and policy-maker in his own right. In a sense, formal organization is an ideology, an interwoven set of ideas prescribing how persons in a given organization should deal with one another. Informal organization, the actual patterns of interaction, are limited by formal organization to varying degrees in different settings.

THE MIDDLE-CLASS PERCEPTUAL SCREEN

When we are dealing with the West Side Organization, this distinction is crucial, for the way the organization actually functions is different from what we might guess. Middle-class people have a tendency to measure organizational efficiency and prestige (without seeing balance sheets) by the relative splendor of the organization's quarters, the behavior of its executives in local and national scenes, the apparent articulateness and efficiency of secretaries and others who are the immediate receptors of communications from outsiders. What is seldom understood by those of us who are part of affluent America is that these expectations are part of our culture, and that there are other cultures in the world, even within our own borders.

The way each of us sees the social, and even the physical, world is very dependent on the way we were raised. In our early years our parents and other authority figures teach us how to react to various people, events, and things in the world. Later on our friends in school teach us, and finally, we are taught by those we live and work with in the adult milieu. Though there are variations among individuals how they are instructed in the ways of society—or "socialized"— there exist patterns characteristic of large segments of the population. Each of these patterns is a way of life—culture or subculture—and each is characterized by a rather well-defined set of expectations about how men deal with each other and how to evaluate these dealings. Each is also characterized by a basic personality, a generalized set of ways of reacting to common social events shared by persons who are members of a given culture or subculture. Each such basic personality is characterized by a distinct "perceptual screen," or set of expectations, that makes it difficult if not impossible for a person to identify social events different from those he is used to seeing or perceiving.

Someone who goes from one culture to another may experience what is popularly called "culture shock," the feeling of derangement and confusion when a person is not able to identify familiar patterns in the new social life surrounding him. Usually when we think about this experience, our referent is a foreign country that is underdeveloped—or bluntly, backward—by our standards. But culture shock can also befall an individual who moves from one way of life to another in the United States—like going from a middle-class district of a city to a lower-class black community, like Chicago's Near West Side.

Most people who make this kind of journey in American social space do not realize that they are moving between different ways of life, between different cultures. And so they are prone to use the same set of expectations they have learned from and applied to their own part of society to evaluate what they see in other parts. People who are serious about coming to understand a different way of life should be willing to undergo the kind of tortuous self-examination required of those who would become psychiatrists and travel into the intimacy of others' minds, or those who would become anthropologists and venture into other ways of life. In order to understand life in the urban, lower-class, black community, the middle-class man must be willing to learn how to evaluate things by the (to him) strange and frightening standards of the black ghetto without losing touch (in madness) with his own world.

Most white people who come to the West Side are not aware that this effort is required of them. Those who are men and women of good will see, according to middle-class standards, sickness, ugliness, squalor, and evil; and on the positive side, only the ability of many to joke about their condition, however bitterly. They miss the fact that in the midst of all they see there is something that is making an important contribution to American life. They miss the fact that these slum dwellers, having been deprived on all the values Americans prize—wealth, status, and power—have, in defense of their humanity, emphasized other values. It is true that these values include violence and crookedness, but others are friendship and affection, brotherhood and charity, and a fundamental commitment to what we loosely call "freedom." American blacks are the only large group of Americans among whom these values are emphasized in fact as well as in thought.

The mistake the white outsider makes in coming to the West Side and in using his own perceptual screen to evaluate what he sees there is very serious indeed, and all but a few make this mistake. Once I saw a very charming and very religious white woman try to convince a young man from the West Side to go back to high school. He was making his living by petty thievery, and when she met him he was drinking wine from a paper cup, which horrified her; the result: no communication. On another occasion some well-intentioned civic leaders came to WSO to talk about the possibility of establishing a police review board to consider allegations of police brutality. They were openly nervous about their physical safety because of the image in their world of West Side blacks as sometime cutthroats—again, an impediment to communication. A number of reporters, some from the most prominent national news organizations, have come to WSO, and seeing the disarray of the WSO office and the flamboyant styles of dress and speech of WSO leaders (by *their* standards) have reported on the organization unfavorably. They missed the point, for even though there are no shiny floors, pretty secretaries, or multi-buttoned telephones, and even though most of the staff members have prison records, even though there is often open drinking in the office—the organization is a smashing success.

FORMAL ORGANIZATION

It is well to keep the middle-class perceptual screen in mind when evaluating WSO and in describing its structure. To the middle-class man, the most familiar and comforting aspect of WSO is its patterns of formal organization and titles. There is a Board of Directors with Archie Hargraves as President. Its meetings are infrequent and the number of members varies, though it has generally been about fifteen or twenty. It is comprised almost entirely of poor people who live in the neighborhood.

The organization has an Executive Director, presently Chester Robinson, who is the effective head and chief policy-making executive of the group. The Director of the Welfare Union, the Executive Director's most important associate, is presently William Darden. Other subordinate positions, each reporting directly to the Executive Director, are the Editor of the *Torch* (now Patricia Stock) and the Chaplain (Robert Strom). The educational and unemployment work of the organization is supervised directly by the Executive Director. Under the Director of the Welfare Union are the Directors of the locals, or branch offices, of the Union. Each of these men has one or two others who work with him part-time.

PATTERNS OF INTRA-ORGANIZATIONAL DEALINGS

All this hierarchy would charm the most ardent designer of organization charts, but it bears little relation to the way the organization functions in terms of daily work patterns. The interaction, while related to the formal structure, is complex and only misleadingly simplified to the hierarchical rhetoric of the organization chart.

The first misunderstanding to be rectified is the notion that Hargraves, in his position as President of the organization and its Board of Directors, is the chief policy-maker of WSO. Though he is held in high regard by members and officers of the organization and participates in some of the discussions on key policy decisions, his voice has increasingly become that of one among equals. He hoped this would happen as the organization grew and developed. His purpose has not been to lead the blacks of the Near West Side, but to stimulate them to take action on their own behalf, gradually phasing himself out of the picture as members of the community begin to feel more competent in speaking and acting for themselves.

Second, the organization is not really hierarchical in structure. The position of Executive Director, now occupied by Robinson, has always been a precarious one. With other strong personalities in the organization, decisions and suggestions from Robinson have frequently been disputed by others. Further, some members of the executive staff have important connections outside the organization that enhance their position in WSO and in the Near West Side community. For example, Darden has participated in several national conferences on welfare and civil rights, has traveled to Mississippi to participate in demonstrations, and is a member of a loosely organized decision-making consortium of Chicago civil rights leaders. Robinson has also participated in outside activities and in addition has been featured in local and national radio and television interviews. Because many strong personalities whose prestige is independent of WSO perform in the leadership structures of the organization, the chief pattern of the leadership of WSO has been internal conflict and change—and this has been more beneficial than detrimental, for no one has become so frustrated as to be alienated from the organization's goals.

Third, the position of key white people in the organization, Robert Strom (Chaplain) and Patricia Stock (Editor of the *Torch*) is difficult to explain. They are at once trusted collaborators—both have certainly been important leaders—but at the same time their motives and feelings are viewed with a certain suspicion by others in the organization. But because both whites and blacks in positions of leadership are aware that a certain amount of suspicion of this kind is unavoidable, and of the deep historical roots of such suspicion, the relationship is healthy, even though strained.

Meetings

COMMUNITY PUBLIC MEETINGS

WSO holds two kinds of meetings open to the community —those held every Wednesday night, and special meetings held to discuss matters of great urgency.

The regular Wednesday night meetings are usually attended by fifty to a hundred neighborhood residents, including some of adolescents, and a handful of people from other parts of town—primarily social workers from the central city and friends from the suburbs. Significantly, no one of known leftist bent attends regularly, though a few have come by from time to time. Such people have always been regarded with suspicion, both because they often attempt to exploit black people for their own purposes (which bear little relation to most of the purposes of WSO) and because many of them simply do not understand life in the black community.

The meetings are run by John Crawford, head of a Welfare Union local, who customarily begins by leading the group in a few "freedom songs," the now familiar derivatives of spirituals that emphasize sacrifice for the sake of the advancement of black Americans.

Following the singing, in which all but a very few participate with gusto, there is generally a speaker—Crawford, Darden, Robinson, or someone else. On two separate occasions Martin Luther King and Stokely Carmichael spoke to gatherings of more than five hundred people. The speeches usually stress self-help and responsible social and political participation, on the one hand, and deplore irresponsible actions, such as selling one's vote or spying for the Democratic political machine, on the other. Interruptions from the audience frequently develop into heated exchanges. Leaders of the organization are criticized and called on to defend themselves. New programs and opportunities are often announced at these meetings. The meetings thus provide an additional formal mechanism for relating the organization to the community—beyond the employment and other services offered on a daily basis.

The vagueness of organizational membership is shown here. There are membership cards and nominal dues paid by many members of the community, but anyone can come to these meetings and can stand and speak his mind, whether or not he is technically a member. (The organization has between two and three thousand formal members.) The open meetings are a healthy kind of relation with the community because they tone down the differentiation between insiders, or members, and outsiders, or nonmembers, making it easier for the organization to be seen and used as a device to facilitate expression by anyone in the community who has something to contribute or a complaint to make.

The other sort of meeting is *ad hoc* and is held to deal with a crisis. Such meetings have been very few in number. The several most important such gatherings in WSO's brief history were associated with the Centennial Laundry crisis, where agendas were prepared and agreements reached after much open discussion among leaders and others. These kinds of meeting will continue to be called in the future to meet crisis situations.

Community meetings serve primarily to politicize mem-

bers of the community who would not otherwise be aware
of WSO's work and problems, a function whose importance
is difficult to overstate. They also serve to provide nonleaders
from the community with an opportunity to participate in
the discussion of organization goals and purposes, but as
with such meetings in most political organizations, the effect of participation is more symbolic than real in terms
of influencing policy.

STRATEGY MEETINGS

Inside. The most important people in the organization
meet frequently to deal with immediate and long-range
problems. The meetings are informal, private, very frank,
and frequently rough. The most common topics on the
agendas are alternatives for action in an immediate crisis,
questions of finance, and questions of how to relate to other
community organizations in Chicago.

During the opening months of WSO the clergymen from
the Urban Training Center had a tendency to dominate the
discussions, particularly Strom and Hargraves. But as the
others have become more confident in their ability to express themselves and more self-assertive, they have become
the central participants, while Strom and Hargraves—in part
purposely, in part by gentle pressure—have been phased out
of their former positions of great influence.

Outside. WSO leaders attend many meetings with other
black leaders in Chicago. They sat in the decision-making
councils that organized the marches sponsored by Martin
Luther King in the summer of 1966 through all-white suburbs to protest discriminatory real estate policies by govern-

ment and private organizations. They have met with other
organizations, such as JOIN and TWO,[3] that are working
on welfare grievances and housing code violations.

WSO has always taken an independent tack in these
meetings, because it is extremely wary of forming coalitions
that may result in having some outsider develop a substantial amount of influence on what WSO will do on the Near
West Side. WSO leaders have from time to time exercised
strong leadership in giving direction to cooperative efforts
in the black freedom movement in Chicago.

Summary: Organization and Outcomes

WSO conducts many activities to protect the members of
the Near West Side community (and certain other communities) from the public and private bureaucracies, which in
the past they dealt with as unguarded individuals. It has
provided jobs, and the motivation to become employed, for
those who were previously without hope. It has removed
many from the welfare rolls, but at the same time it has
worked hard to protect those on welfare from victimization
by public officials. It has provided a limited educational
program for the community and published a community
newspaper. All of these services have been without charge
to their beneficiaries.

In addition, WSO leaders have become prominent figures
in the local and national manifestations of the nascent black
freedom movement, serving on informal steering commit-
tees and participating in demonstrations and in other more

3. JOIN is Jobs Or Income Now; TWO is The Woodlawn Organization. More is said on both organizations in Chapter 6.

formal attempts to articulate the interests of the black community to city and state authorities.

In short, though the organization has participated in efforts aimed at securing high-level outcomes from the political system, such as an open housing ordinance or integrated schools, its major emphasis has been on low-level outcomes of direct concern to individuals.

It has made impressive advances utilizing styles of organization and participation elicited from the members of the community, rather than forced on them by outsiders interested in remolding West Side styles and personalities in their own images. These facts sum to a most impressive kind of outcome—a change in the style of politics of the West Side black community, earlier dominated by middle-class adherents to the political and criminal syndicates, a change in which the poor and black have begun very effectively to speak for themselves.

This quiet break with the past now taking place in many localities will have consequences yet unimagined by most students of contemporary American politics.

PART

IV

DEFINITION AND REDEFINITION

6

DEFINITIONS AND
OLD POLICIES FOR CHANGE

The Importance of Definitions

According to many writers America is presently on the brink of a period of change, one that will have a significant impact on American life for many decades to come.

Many of the efforts of the men and women who seek this change are built on common definitions of what is at stake and of what is required to effect change. Who is the wolf, and who the sheep? Who is master, and who the slave? Who are the villains? These are questions of definition, and definitions in many circumstances are political and important, for they determine who we are, who we may become, what we may do. They are especially important in thinking about the West Side Organization and about what is going on in America.

THE PUBLIC AND PRIVATE REVOLUTIONS

The nature of the period we are in, or are about to be in, is disputed, but most thinkers argue in the language of aggregates, and only a few address themselves except in a cursory way to the individual as he confronts his fellows. In this way they view the change (or revolution), whatever else it may be, as essentially a public phenomenon, as a set of shifts in the lives of groups and categories of Americans.

In opposition to this view, the WSO leaders see that the revolution must necessarily be substantially private— concerned with changes in individuals. Yet they see changes in individuals as having social significance, and sometimes appear to ignore the effects of large events, such as making laws and electing officials. But both WSO leaders and social analysts who think primarily in terms of aggregates address themselves to the same social circumstances—the configuration of American life in the second half of the twentieth century. Both consider private and public aspects of the issues and possible revolution that surround us. But the definitions of problems and the corresponding modes of action and analysis that WSO sees are markedly different from those of analysts and actors who are preoccupied with large events such as huge demonstrations, civil rights acts, and the appointment of Negroes to high office.

SOCIAL CHANGE, ACTION, AND DEFINITIONS

The meaning of social change. "Social change" can mean many things. The definition given to it determines what can be seen as problematic. If social change (in the context of the modern world) is the transformation of predominantly agricultural societies into predominantly industrial ones, the problems of any underdeveloped country may be seen as the technical problems associated with engineering that transformation. Similarly, if social change is the outcome of struggles between classes of human beings in a given society, what may be seen as problematic is limited to questions of whether or not such struggles can take place in the absence of violence, of how socially valued goods (such as good housing and leisure time) are to be redistributed among classes, and so on.

There are as many postures toward the problems of societal transformations as there are definitions of social change. What is seen as problematic is almost entirely a function of the definition employed. And such definitions, following the sociologists of knowledge, are largely a function of the social settings in which they arise.

Perspectives and definitions. For this reason the definitions of social change, in the context of contemporary America, utilized by WSO, an example of a lower-class black political organization, and those used by the major political actors in America are bound to be different. And the things each sees as problems are bound to be different as well.

"The establishment"[1] sees the major dimension of social change in contemporary America as the orderly incorporation of outsiders over an extended period of time into full

1. This term is used to designate the various elites of society. Certainly members of these elites are occupied with what they regard as their pluralism, their divisions and differences. But viewed from the bottom, from WSO, the divisions and differences disappear, and the term "establishment" becomes more meaningful than in other contexts.

participation in the American way of life—as assimilation. Its historical imagination is heavily laden with remembrances: of the American Revolution as an important blow struck for freedom, setting an example for the French Revolution, which followed almost immediately; of the freeing of the slaves by Abraham Lincoln; of the battle against Communism waged by the American national government in many parts of the world in recent years. It sees social change in America as the gradual uplifting of various racial and ethnic groups to higher standards of living—and to increased Americanization. As a result, it sees the "Negro problem" in America as one of prejudice and discrimination (and not of oppression), similar to the prejudice and discrimination experienced by various European minorities on their arrival to this country earlier in this century and before. From this viewpoint the problem is how to construct programs and pass legislation that will open doors, increase skills, and re-educate—all to hasten the process of assimilation.

The view of the oppressed black people in American cities, as manifest in the minds of the leaders of WSO, is entirely different. They see no past glories of America and view it as a racist society, which throughout its history has consistently oppressed and murdered their ancestors and many others all over this planet. Their thinking on the major dimensions of social change in contemporary America centers about the recognition of the racist idea as it permeates American social action at home and elsewhere, and they are wedded to the proposition that individual black men must, as the first step toward freedom, recognize this idea and begin to combat it in their thoughts about themselves and their actions toward others. To a certain extent they de-emphasize questions of programs and of social structures and stress ideas. Every thought and every action, every speech and every conversation, is devoted, at least in part, to combatting the idea that blacks are inferior to whites.

They see social change as the reconstruction of individuals—as the reconstruction of their views of themselves. And therefore, what they see as problematic is very different from what the establishment is enchanted by in building its programs and passing its legislation. Programs of retraining and economic development for black communities are imperative, though they do not in themselves adequately address what WSO sees as the total problem—racism. Racism is not something that can be fought only by programs and laws. Fundamentally, it must be fought in the mind of each man, for himself and others.

Using this principle as a guide, the staff of WSO seeks not so much to find jobs for people or help them in their problems with the welfare bureaucracy, as it does to change their minds about themselves. WSO leaders regard finding jobs and settling welfare grievances as victories, as do members of the establishment. But they consider these victories meaningless if their beneficiaries do not in the process come to regard themselves differently—as black people with a rich heritage and the right to the same level of material life enjoyed by white people, not as niggers begging favors from the state.

Views and actions. So programs of retraining in the skills of industry do not adequately speak to the problem as seen by the lower-class black communities of America. When the instructors and administrators in these programs present themselves to their students as doing them a favor, they damage their teaching irreparably, for the students see in them yet another set of racists—like the teachers, policemen, and social workers who have gone before. This sense has caused some blacks to refuse to participate in such programs, and others to drop out once enrolled.

Similarly, the passage of civil rights legislation does not speak to the problems as seen by many members of the lower-class black community, for none of the civil rights legislation has made any difference whatever to them. They are concerned not with what the government says should happen to them as they confront employers, shopkeepers, real estate men, and city schools, but with what *in fact* happens to them in their daily lives. And it still amounts to the same old thing, in spite of the celebrated advances of recent years. If anything, this legislation has made them more cynical about white people and the Negroes in their charge, for they have laid bare the trickery; they have seen that this legislation is largely symbolic in content.

I do not mean that the officials of American governments and private organizations have purposely avoided the problems of the black community. To the contrary, they have addressed themselves in a very responsible way to what *they* see as the problems. It is tragic that they do not see that the black community is in some respects a different world from theirs. It is unfortunate that they are not able to see what they have done and continue to do to the black people of America.

It is as difficult for white people to escape being oppressors as it is for blacks to escape being oppressed—and both battles must be waged by each man in his own mind.

GOALS AND ACTIONS—THE PROBLEM OF EVALUATION

What problems are seen depends on how one defines social change, on how one looks at America and at its black community. Who is to determine what views of social change, of America, and of the black community are to prevail? Who is to decide which construction of the condition of the black man in America will be used as the cornerstone of public policy? This is quite clearly a political issue, an issue of power. And equally clearly, the construction of the establishment will prevail unless blacks can do something to change its way of thinking.

One way of altering the mentality of the establishment is to evaluate its programs, and members of the black community are bound to evaluate the War-on-Poverty and civil-rights programs of the various American national and local governments one way or another. One method is with the bomb. You approve of something, you leave it alone; you disapprove, you blow it up.[2] Other, more ordinary methods include the use of the electoral process, the formation of interest groups, and so on.

It is at this juncture that the differences in definitions are crucial. The ways black men will evaluate government programs are determined by the establishment, by those responsible for the formulation of the programs. Little heed is paid to the peaceful efforts to reformulate the role of black people in America; remember, the laws and programs passed so far have made little difference to the vast majority of blacks,

2. So far there have been periods of violent insurrection in the black ghettoes of more than a hundred American cities.

though the pressures for these programs have been exerted largely through the normal channels of interest groups and electoral process.

Whose goals? What needs to happen in order to avoid the translation of peaceful demands into violent ones? The goals of the people in the lower-class black community and their way of looking at the social world are different from those of the middle-class molders of programs for the ghetto. The programmers and legislators must make a substantial effort to uncover these differences and develop programs to meet the demands of the black community.

Whose action? There are many paths to achieving any set of goals. There are bound to be many paths to achieving the goals of the black community. And the actions taken in pursuit of the goals of the black community may be carried on by the establishment and its representatives, or by leaders of the black community, or by both. The most direct route the goals of the people who live in the West Sides of America is through their own actions on their own behalf, for this action gets to the central problem of racism directly. Moves controlled or directed by others implicitly designate black people as inferior and incapable of acting on their own behalf.

Whose evaluation? And further, the only meaningful evaluations of programs for the black community are those of its residents. Unless they are able to indicate whether or not changes or attempts at change please them, no one will ever know that a program has gone wrong until it is too late, until the bomb comes crashing through the window. For strangers to design programs allegedly to help members of the black community and then to evaluate the programs themselves is dangerous in the face of the vast disparity between how the blacks and the establishment see the problems of black people.

These are not easy problems, and they are urgent ones. Again, the actions (or inactions) of the public and private bureaucracies of America directed at black communities will be evaluated in one way or another by blacks. The choice of the way is up to those in power, not the blacks.

The Public Definition and Its Consequences

Many attempts to build political organizations in lower-class communities have been based on the establishment view of what is problematic in these materially destitute parts of American cities. These organizations are built on ordinary definitions of social change and of the condition of lower-class black people. These definitions of social change in contemporary America may be designated as public, as they direct our attention to changes in the situations of aggregates of individuals, rather than to changes in individuals' personalities.

The most fundamental error of these organizational efforts is their assertion of the *myth of community organization*, derived directly from the ordinary, public definitions of social change and the problems of urban black people.

ORGANIZATIONS

Almost daily we read in the news that X citizens' group has done Y action in pursuit of its aims, Y being any number of things: endorsing a candidate for public office, a demonstration, a strike. In the political culture of America we believe in organizations. Citizens, it is said, have the right to petition the government—through their organizations—for the redress of grievances. Even in the nineteenth century, Alexis de Tocqueville noted that Americans were the most organization conscious people in his experience.

When we think about organizations, we think about membership: bodies of citizens united in support of their common interests; and we think about officials of organizations; and perhaps about offices or buildings. But organization is a difficult concept to define. Is it its members? What its members do? Its officers? What its officers do? March and Simon, in one of the most distinguished books on organizations, write: "It is easier, and probably more useful, to give examples of . . . organizations than to define the term."[3] But in falling back on the use of examples to define the concept of organization, we are left with vague thoughts of members, officials, and buildings much in our minds as we contemplate organizations.

COMMUNITY ORGANIZATIONS

Building from this vagueness, and thinking about what is loosely called "community organization," we can only become even more ambiguous. Community organizations are thought to be bands of citizens of particular parts of our villages and cities working to pursue what they see as their common interests. In one of the most articulate of the usual

3. James G. March and Herbert Simon, *Organizations* (Wiley, 1958), p. 1.

definitions of community organization, Murray G. Ross writes:

> Community organization [is] a process by which a community identifies its needs or objectives, orders (or ranks) these needs or objectives, develops the confidence and will to work at these needs or objectives, finds the resources (internal and/or external) to deal with these needs or objectives, takes action in respect to them, and in so doing extends and develops cooperative and collaborative attitudes and practices in the community.[4]

But whether a community is considered to be geographically based (having a membership of individuals who reside in some particular part of a village or city), or functionally based (having a membership of individuals sharing common interests, such as a labor union), there may be a diversity of membership and interests in it and a number of possible sets of "needs or objectives" that could be identified.

Suppose some of these sets of needs and objectives or the means to attain them are contradictory. Taking an example of the first, suppose the middle-class residents of a geographic area are interested in urban renewal, in tearing down substandard dwellings and replacing them with middle-class housing (at middle-class prices), while the lower-class residents are interested in repairing the existing structures or in constructing lower-class housing (at lower-class prices) to replace them. What is the community interest? What are the community's needs and objectives—the construction of middle-class housing or lower-class, or both? Taking an example of the second, a possible contradiction

4. Murray G. Ross, *Community Organization* (Harper and Row, 1955), p. 39.

in means, suppose the church ministers in an area who have friendly relations with local political officials are less interested in challenging those officials, because of possibly jeopardizing these relations, than are local militant groups who are not on speaking terms with officials. Does the community interest lie in challenging the political officials, or not?

VALUE-FREE COMMUNITY ORGANIZATION:

ALINSKY, THE MASTER MYTH-MAKER

Clearly there is bound to be conflict in any incipient geographic or functional community over the nature of its interests. The best (or most powerful) politicians in the community will win; the others will lose. Until recently in the black communities of many American cities, certainly in Chicago, the winners have been the representatives of political machines, ghetto merchants, the police, the gangsters (who are white, or managed by whites).

Saul Alinsky, a self-styled radical, has taken to the business of what he calls community organization.[5] For a high price he will take a team of "community organizers" into a relatively small area of a city and "organize" it. Building on extant organizations that have few links to the rest of the city (not, for example, the representatives of the urban political machine), he seeks to form "an organization of organizations" supposed to find the community interest and represent it to the central urban government. Put differently, he seeks to change the game so that different politicians in the community win—so that the "organization of

5. Alinsky's style of community organization is discussed in Charles E. Silberman's *Crisis in Black and White* (Random House, 1964), pp. 321–328.

organizations" instead of the old-line politicians comes to define the community interest.

Prominent in the thoughts of writers on community organization, such as Ross, are the notions that, somehow, some communities are not organized, and that the enterprise of organizing them is simply a matter of pulling together forces dormant in the community into a cohesive political organization that can find and articulate the community interests. But in reality all ghetto communities are already organized, and anyone who would start a basic effort to build a new political organization—whether in the style of Alinsky or not —is engaged not in community organization, but in community *reorganization.*

In any reorganization of a part of the political configuration of a city, new powers will come to determine and articulate goals. While it is clear that the old elite (again, usually the standard ghetto proprietors: police, merchants, gangsters, politicians) will be replaced, not everyone else —not the remainder of the community—will replace them. Only a few will win, while very many will continue to lose.

Herein lies the myth of community organization. First, there is no such thing as community disorganization, at least not in the lower-class black communities in America —these are tightly organized and controlled by their proprietors. Therefore, community organization is really community reorganization. And, second, there is no possible way to reorganize a ghetto so that all the possible interests (save those to be defeated in any reorganization effort) can triumph when these interests conflict.

In the face of these facts, Alinsky seems to suggest that value-free (or neutral) community organization is possible and to present his efforts as such. Certainly almost any reorganization is preferable to the continued dominance of the ancient proprietors of urban black communities, but different subgroups of the community prefer some alternatives to others. Alinsky offers only one possibility, the assertion of the influence of those in the community who bear the badges of middle-class respectability—the ministers, the shopkeepers (nongouging variety), the doctors, the boys clubs. What most of us think of as the destitute, the criminal, the deviant, the unusual are left out. And in many urban black communities this group is a majority. Surely some other kind of reorganization would be better from the perspective of this majority. Alinsky has made it clear that he believes that only usual kinds of people are qualified to formulate goals and to articulate them; only the middle-class minority is qualified to rule.

The Woodlawn Organization. The Woodlawn Organization (TWO) is the most famous of Alinsky's children, and the best known and best financed of all the black community organizations in Chicago.[6] Alinsky started it in 1960 at the invitation of some community leaders, mostly clergymen, in Chicago's predominantly black Woodlawn section, near the University of Chicago campus on the South Side of the city. Employing his usual style, Alinsky formed "an organization of organizations" whose components were prominent existing businesses and associations in Woodlawn. As it grew, this federation began to include not only church organizations and civic groups, but also business-

6. For a description of The Woodlawn Organization and its growth, see Charles E. Silberman, *Crisis in Black and White* (Random House, 1964), pp. 318–350.

men's associations and other groups. According to plan, this umbrella organization became increasingly cohesive as the result of intensive interaction among its members. It is supposed to be controlled by the people who live in the area —as opposed to those who work there and live elsewhere. It is supposed to present unified community postures on public issues to the urban political arena, in particular, to the officials at City Hall.

TWO has accomplished much. It has changed decisions at City Hall on the location and nature of slum clearance programs—cynically known in Chicago and elsewhere as "Negro removal." In the view of many it has provided militant community leadership that articulates community interests independent of the old proprietors of Woodlawn. It is seen as having provided new channels of communication in the community so that businessmen and ministers, priests and politicians, find it easy to discourse on subjects of mutual interest. It has given many people in the community a new sense of participation in shaping their own destinies. All of these changes are laudable.

But they are misleading. First of all, Alinsky was invited by local community leaders. Those who were most likely to know about Alinsky and to have the skills and confidence required to make such an invitation were accustomed to dealing in the white man's world in the white man's symbols. They were predominantly members of the black middle class of Woodlawn. Once they assumed leadership in soliciting outside help, they set the pattern for the evolution of the leadership structures of the local political reorganization (the results of Alinsky's efforts). This progression was cumulative: the people who could invite Alinsky were the people who could raise the money to finance Alinsky's work, and these were the people who ended up in positions of leadership and control in the organization.

Second, these community leaders are, at best, articulating what they perceive to be the primary interests of the community, and these are often not the interests of the impoverished black man present in such great numbers in Woodlawn. To this man TWO is often another "front job for the white folks." In its emphasis on middle-class leadership TWO is not structured to discover the interests of this man. And even if it were, it would be unlikely that it could articulate them. Only this man himself can adequately speak for his interests. He will speak one way or another, either peaceably or with Molotov cocktails and bullets. Again, the choice is up to those in control; in Woodlawn, that is, in part, TWO.

Alinsky's projects of social reorganization place heavy emphasis on the reification of social institutions that are ghetto images of what predominates in white society: churches, formal and informal political organizations, businessmen's societies, and so on. Before 1960 these were not the social institutions that predominated in Woodlawn, and to strengthen them was to augment the influence of their leaders and followers in Woodlawn compared to others in the community. And while these "others" may include the previously dominant proprietors of Woodlawn, most "others" in the community are those who are least likely to participate in any of the usual types of social institutions. The man who is poor and black is presented with yet another figure, however black, to tell the world what he wants.

Though the achievements of TWO are impressive, the organization has not made a fundamental change in the lives and outlook of the majority who occupy the bottom social ranks of Woodlawn. It may be imagined that from their perspective TWO seems at best a misguided social innovation, at worst enlightened colonialism.

THE CIVIL RIGHTS MOVEMENT

The civil rights movement is another source of strategies for reorganizing political relationships within black communities and between black communities and the society they are imbedded in. There are many different perspectives on political organization and political theory in the civil rights movement; indeed, the movement itself is not a single social movement, but many, each with its own ideas and brand of protest, though there may be substantial overlap among the organizations and ideologies involved. But an area of sharpest disagreement is the matter of goals, which only recently has been discussed in a meaningful way. Some say that the goal is not assimilation but separation, while others stay with the traditional quest for inclusion, and still others say that the question of separation or inclusion is not the first question, but how to improve the economic position of black people in America.

In contrast, a commonality among these movements is their reliance on demonstrations. While demonstrations may achieve some changes in the political order, and while they may indeed change the minds of black and white alike about the alleged inferiority of blacks, they are not enough in themselves to cause a reordering of society. They will not, in the analytical style of WSO, alter the predominance of racism in society. A demonstration may get the Cook County Department of Public Aid to release a check for a welfare recipient who was unjustly deprived of his allotment, but no one can demonstrate every day for each of the welfare recipients who is done wrong. Any serious effort at alleviating such injustices must include plans for training welfare recipients to handle their complaints themselves, with no help from anyone either in demonstration or counsel. And this is the difficult work in community reorganization—the reorientation of the personalities of blacks and others in the vast nation of the destitute in America. The notion implicit in much activity of these civil rights movements is that if one demonstrates, somehow community reorganization will follow naturally—a serious miscalculation.

SDS/JOIN

Another perspective on the reorganization of political structures in the neighborhoods of the urban poor is that of JOIN, an organization whose clientele is almost exclusively the newly arrived poor from white Appalachia on Chicago's North Side.

One of JOIN's parents is the Students for a Democratic Society (SDS), a national organization of American students tagged in the national press as one of a constellation of "New Left" organizations in American politics. In recent years the leadership of SDS has focused its attention increasingly on the politics of the poor—in addition to its spectacular concern with American foreign policy and its efforts to remake the American university—seeking to alter the political organization of slum communities in many American cities, among them Newark, Cleveland, and Chicago. Each of the efforts has a style of its own, though there are themes binding them together as the offspring of a single set of ideas.

Only the Chicago project is discussed here. It is called Jobs Or Income Now (JOIN) and has been in operation since the winter of 1964–65. The project has de-emphasized the SDS name since that organization has taken on an increasingly radical national image, but the people who started the JOIN project and many who presently staff it as volunteers and paid workers are members and friends of SDS, though many local poor people participate in key decision-making processes.

Located in an area peopled primarily by poor whites from various parts of the rural South and Appalachia, it has not been spectacular in its activities or achievements. Financed mostly by contributions and membership dues from the neighborhood, JOIN has concentrated on eliminating abuses by welfare officials and slum landlords, though it also engages in other activities. Its style emphasizes demonstrations and mass meetings, though a certain amount of hard administrative work is apparently carried out by staff members who process welfare and housing grievances.

Its major weakness is that the SDS members who are its backbone seem more concerned with theatrical forms of political participation and with training the neighborhood poor in SDS thoughts on the alleged benefits of such action than with the hard work involved in eliciting the political participation of the poor in whatever style the poor themselves may choose.

In this way the North Side JOIN project has much in common with the South Side TWO community organization. JOIN has sought *explicitly* to provide an impoverished community with a new political style and ideology, while TWO has done so *implicitly*, since the ascendance of middle-class blacks has been the necessary outcome of Alinsky's way of working with the poor.

The difference between the two is simple: up to the cut-off date of this report the JOIN project has largely been a failure. Visiting the organization's storefront headquarters, you can usually hear any number of true believers and permanent sophomores discourse on the great things being done by the poor in the neighborhood, on how they are finally finding their natural ideology and beginning to take their place in Chicago politics—an ideology and place strangely akin to what is heard in the speeches of SDS leaders. But the accomplishments of the organization in achieving alterations in political outcomes important to the poor are not impressive—both in changing grand policy made at City Hall and elsewhere and in handling welfare and housing grievances. This is not to say that JOIN has had no success; only that the success has not been as significant as the noise of marches and demonstrations might lead one to think. The TWO project, on the other hand, has achieved many important alterations in political outcomes, even though the political efforts of the organization are based on the perceptions of its middle-class leaders of the needs and interests of the poor, which are frequently inaccurate.

Conclusion

The public definition of social change leads to the kinds of ideology that has guided The Woodlawn Organization, many parts of the civil rights movement, and JOIN. Though this thinking differs in many ways, they have one common theme. All prescribe directing the major attentions of any organizing effort at those who are in power in the political system, rather than at those who are not. The organizing efforts of all three types seek to manipulate impoverished human beings in presentations to the authorities in the hope that policies will be changed. And quite clearly, the concern with policies—the actions and representations of power-holders—is a direct derivative of the public definition of social change. This definition would have us direct our attentions at large events—at systems, at aggregates.

The Woodlawn Organization and many civil rights efforts have endeavored to secure changes in urban renewal plans, to elect social reformers and radicals to public office, to pass legislation. In contrast, the JOIN effort at first encounter does not appear to fit so easily into the same category. But while the JOIN organizers talk of the "grass roots," of outcasts, of oppression, their actions are not consonant with their rhetoric. While their speech would have us believe that they wish to elicit the political participation of the poor in their own style, they have tried to indoctrinate the poor with the JOIN understanding of conditions of social life in America.

Taking these efforts as representative of the most prominent styles seeking to alter the participation of the poor in American society, efforts to reorganize the poor—especially to reorganize the poor and black—have failed to cast off the web of oppression binding so many of the poor in America. This is not to say that they have failed altogether. To the contrary, they have had remarkable successes promoting the kinds of changes prescribed if one thinks of social change as a public phenomenon.

The private, WSO, definition of social change is different

from the public definition that has been the paradigm within which the programs of the TWO's, the JOIN's, and the civil rights movements have been formulated. And consequently, its actions are different.

7

THE MESSAGE:
A REDEFINITION

What is happening in the West Side Organization, and in the minds of the men who run it, may be a social innovation representing America's last chance before it breaks apart in chronic violent revolution, waged by black people and their allies in the assertion of their humanity.

In thinking about this possibility, I begin with the individual. Specifically, I begin with the oppressed personality and the way it is produced in society.

For some considerable time students of man have wondered why people of low social status, who are often deprived of what most believe to be the bare necessities of human existence, do not revolt.[1] Their passiveness is usually explained by the concept of legitimation. Since the

1. For example, see Erich Fromm, *Escape from Freedom* (Holt, 1941) and Robert E. Lane, "The Fear of Equality," *American Political Science Review*, LIII (1959), pp. 35–51.

inequities in society (which in severe cases may be called oppression) cannot conceivably be maintained by coercion (there is not a policeman for each one of us), these inequities must somehow be legitimized; that is, citizens must come to accept them without the use of violence by the authorities.[2] They must be *trained to believe* that inequities and oppression are morally right or at least unavoidable.

The legitimation of oppression is effected through the adherence of the populace to ideas that explicitly or implicitly support it. These ideas constitute the ideology of a given society, the thoughts most citizens accept without examination as being correct descriptive, prescriptive, and explanatory statements about social matters. For example, we all believe in freedom, equality, and justice, and almost all of us believe that if these words do not describe present American society, there is an even chance that they will sometime in the proximate future. We disagree about the proper definitions of these terms—does freedom require that I sell my house to a Jew? But almost all of us agree that freedom is a good and attainable thing, whatever it is; few would dare propose that it is undesirable or unattainable.

Most of the arguments and violent conflicts that take place in industrial society are over the definition of terms that we all accept and even celebrate as symbols.[3] In few cases are conflicts structured around fundamental criticisms of societies and of their ideologies. Seldom are alternative concepts offered as replacements for those forming the cornerstones of societal ideologies.

2. Harold D. Lasswell argues this point well, though he does not use the word "legitimacy," in Chapter 2 of *Politics: Who Gets What, When, How* (World, 1958; first published 1938).

3. Karl Mannheim, *Ideology and Utopia* (Harcourt, 1965; first published 1936), pp. 23, 56.

The presence, acceptance, and promotion of a given ideology in society obviously have consequences for the individuals who are its members. For whether or not we agree
on the definitions of ideological concepts, our acceptance
of the symbols (words) as the infrastructure of our world
view limits the possible ways we may view ourselves and
our surroundings.[4]

If we accept freedom, equality, and justice as fundamental in the way we examine our own governments and those
of other cultures, ironically we have made the first step
toward the acceptance of oppression. The second and crucial step is seeing these concepts as accurate descriptions
of American society of the moment. Once this is done, most
people find it very difficult to entertain the possibility that
some categories of individuals in our society are oppressed.
(After all, if it is an open system, everyone deserves what
he gets.) This accedence has serious consequences for everyone, of whatever social status and style of life: those who
are rich and/or respected believe themselves to be superior;
those who are poor and/or despised (oppressed) believe
themselves to be inferior.[5]

It is the poor and despised who concern me here. What
are the personal consequences of the American ideology
for the poor and despised? Or put differently, what is the
nature of the oppressed personality in America—in particular the poor residents of urban black communities? And
what is necessary if such personalities are to become polit-

4. The roots of ideological commitment run deep into the structures
of societies. The Chinese "brainwashing" efforts on prisoners of the
Korean War bear this out. See Edgar H. Schein, "Reaction Patterns to
Severe, Chronic Stress in American Army Prisoners of War of the
Chinese," *Journal of Social Issues*, XIII (1957), pp. 21–30.

5. Bernard Berelson and Gary A. Steiner, *Human Behavior* (Harcourt, 1964), p. 489.

ical in articulating demands for a dramatic uplifting of urban black people in America? In short, what is the genius of WSO?

The Individual and Social Change

Before these questions can be answered using the WSO experience, we must confront some basic questions of how individuals are related to society: the oppressed personality and the individual meaning of social change must be examined.

Social change is an ambiguous concept; as I have said, it has been defined in many divergent ways. It may be thought of as systemic, involving a modification of society as a whole; for example, the phenomenon of industrialization. It may be thought of as cultural, involving a fundamental reorientation in the values in a given society; for example, the change from feudalism to the nation-state as the organizational theme of European political life in the middle ages. It may be thought of as involving more limited changes in society, such as the recent addition of women to the voting rolls in Western countries. It may be thought of as an individual and personal phenomenon: what changes take place in individual personalities and classes of personalities? Or it may be considered as a complex combination of modifications in both society and individual—even in the way individual and society are related. This final possibility is, for the purposes of this essay, the most attractive because it allows us to think in societal terms without a depersonalization in the analysis in which the individual is lost.

THE INDIVIDUAL IN SOCIETY

Culture and personality. Two further ambiguous concepts are *culture* and *personality*. But their ambiguity, like that of social change, does not substantially limit their intuitive utility for analysis. These concepts are intimately related, though not always within the work of a single writer. Mc-Clelland defines personality "as the most adequate conceptualization of a person's behavior in all its detail that the scientist can give at a moment in time."[6] Very loosely then, an individual's personality is what we think he is like; it is the patterns we see in his behavior. Linked closely to this notion is culture, defined by one writer as "the abstracted nonbiological conditions of human life."[7] "All cultures are largely made up of overt, patterned ways of behaving, feeling, and reacting."[8] Here is the juncture between culture and personality: both are said to consist of *patterns of behaviors*. As we make our way through the world, we come upon tribesmen and strangers. Tribesmen are identified to us by certain patterns in their behaviors that are familiar to us, patterns learned in the daily life of family and community.

Language, a key. The most obvious pattern of behavior by which we may distinguish tribesmen from strangers is language. Germans speak German, and Hausa speak Hausa. Yet even within a single language in a single country there

6. David C. McClelland, *Personality* (Holt, 1951), p. 69.
7. Berelson and Steiner, p. 644.
8. Alfred L. Kroeber and Clyde Kluckhohn, "Culture: A Critical Review of Concepts and Definitions," *Papers of the Peabody Museum*, XLVII (1952), p. 157.

are different languages. There are different kinds of American English. Even within the bounds of a single American city, Chicago, for example, people who live in different suburbs speak in slightly different ways; and these ways differ from those of the Gold Coast inhabitants, the upper-class apartment buildings and town houses along Lake Michigan; and these are still different from the speech of the residents of the South Side and West Side black communities.

A black man coming to the Near West Side is not immediately regarded as an insider. But what most quickly identifies him as an insider and ingratiates him with the local residents is a command of the local style of speech. It is different from much of what is spoken in affluent Chicago not only in vocabulary and inflection, but in its structure and ethos. It is not enough simply to master the vocabulary, inflection, and logic of this brand of American English; one must acquire some understanding of the way of life this language belongs to.

It seems simple and crude upon first encounter because its vocabulary is limited in terms of legitimate words in the more familiar brands of American English, while it is rich in what is thought of as slang. Many words are pronounced differently, what some would call wrong and slurred. Furthermore, many statements seem empty and irrelevant. Yet when we think of it not as an aberration of familiar American English but as a foreign language with its own logic and cultural roots, the language appears to offer a richness in possibilities for expressiveness unknown in familiar American English.[9]

9. Since anthropologists have long argued that there is no such thing as a simple language, we should be suspicious of our sentiments when we think of lower class brands of American English as simpler

The differences between West Side English and familiar American English are important, since by examining them we can find clues to the differences in the cultures of the urban affluent and the West Side, (that is, the cultures of urban residents who are black and poor). And from these clues the nature of the oppressed personality can be derived, for language and personality are closely related.

Compared to most kinds of urban middle-class English, West Side English boasts more words and expressions that may be used to curse, threaten, or mock others; there are more expressions to evoke laughter or good feeling; and the kinesic code of the language of gestures is very different.[10] These are the chief distinguishing characteristics of the language from casual observation. Yet in these distinctions it is possible to begin to see the differences between the culture of the black and poor in Chicago and the cultures of many others.

First, the fact that the language is rich in pejoratives suggests that obvious violence, both verbal and physical, may

---

than others. The importance of language in the transmission of culture is in itself ample evidence for this. See A. I. Hallowell, "Culture, Personality, and Society," in *Anthropology Today*, A. L. Kroeber, ed. (University of Chicago Press, 1953).

10. There is an enormous variety of "mother fuckers" of every imaginable meaning and inflection, for example. And the use of humorous similes is common—for example, in the laughing comparison of certain brutal policemen to ridiculous cowboy movie heroes. Also the modification of the usual inflection of ordinary phrases is used to transform them into new expressions with humorous meanings. For example, the meaning of "He was a *bad* stud," is altered drastically by changing the emphasis to "He was a *baaaad* stud." West Siders think the handshake is boring and execute it without enthusiasm, if at all. The more common gesture of greeting is a subtle motion or posturing of the whole body accompanied by the question, "What's *to* it?"

play a more important part in the daily life of the West Side than in the middle and upper classes. In this extremely impoverished quarter of the city, obvious violence is a characteristic way of negotiating disagreements; for everything is in short supply, including human kindness, and disputes are frequent and serious.

Second, that West Side English is rich in expressions of humor and good feeling puts the paradox of West Side life squarely before us. Though human kindness is short, the little bit that exists is serious. No one has very many real friends, and survival requires each person to be suspicious of those who are not his friends. But on the other hand, one will do virtually anything for someone who is his friend—*anything*: lie, rob, even kill; lend money, share living space and food. And much of the language of friendship is that of humor as well.

Expecting people to have something that approximates a uniform approach to the world, it alarms strangers to the West Side that some residents may be extremely hard and violent toward their enemies while they are soft and beautiful to their friends. And in an expression of his bigotry, or to be stylish, "ethnocentrism," the outsider may regard this perceived inconsistency as an indication of confusion, of inferiority.

Yet if we entertain the possibility that the West Side man may be different from many others in American society, we must take another perspective. Life on the West Side may be seen as more serious and demanding than in other parts of American society. The business of friendship and the enterprise of enmity are, therefore, more serious. So one has close friends and close enemies, rather than vague friends and shadowy enemies, as is the case with life in much of the mainstream.

Life is more serious and intense on the West Side, for one is threatened frequently and the retreat permitted to those affluent Americans (who cannot bear to contemplate the possibility of nuclear war, for example) is not permitted to the West Side man, for retreat is paramount to extinction. To disengage yourself from threats is to allow the threats to consume you. And it should be understood that the addiction to drugs and alcohol and the use of marijuana are not a retreat from immediate threats, only a retreat from the overbearing intensity of West Side life.

Finally, the kinesic code of the language of gestures is different. Some people find this difficult to see in watching black people treat with one another. But it is easily seen by all save the most insensitive when lower-class blacks and whites, the two stereotyped opposites in this regard, are viewed as they dance to the same blues music on the same dance floor. With the resurgence of the blues in Chicago, several nightclubs have opened and feature dancing and a blues band of four or five black musicians. Some of these places are in entertainment neighborhoods permitting them a racially mixed clientele. As blacks (many from the lower classes) and whites dance, it is easily seen that the motions and gestures made by black people are generically different from those made by whites: the whites are tense and jerky while the blacks are easy and smooth.

Connecting these two major parts of the language of black people on the West Side, the spoken word and the gesture, is revealing. Examining the spoken language, we find black people more intense than white people; but at the same time in the language of gestures they are smoother and easier, less tight.

Not everyone on the West Side is like this stereotyped sketch—indeed, very few individuals are like it. Yet the stereotype finds its utility in the way it amalgamates characteristics found in abundance among a group of persons, such as the blacks of the West Side. There is no man like the stereotype, yet the stereotype is Everyman.

This description is a celebration of the things I have found exceptional about the men and women of the Near West Side, the good and human things; in no way is it an apology. It is an alternative to the usual view of blacks as lazy and loose, on the one hand, and violent and aggressive, on the other. To the contrary, Everyman of the black community is intensely engaged with life, and it is only through intense engagement that he is able to survive the evil and inhumane conditions that are the bounds within which he has been forced to operate.

THE PERSONALITY OF THE OPPRESSED

It has recently been noted that the crime rate in black communities is higher than in other parts of American cities. Some writers have even stated that most crimes committed by blacks are committed on their fellows.[11] The most perceptive say that the recent insurrections in American cities are directed primarily against shops and people resident in black communities. Herein lies the crucial problem of the oppressed man, of the oppressed personality.

In the space of a single afternoon spent on the West Side,

11. For example, see Phillip H. Ennis, "Crime, Victims and the Police," *Transaction*, IV, No. 7 (1967), pp. 39–40.

it would become apparent to almost any man in America that the people of the West Side live under conditions that consistently deprive them of most of the things Americans contemplate when they turn their minds to the good life. They are without adequate food, clothing, and shelter; their children go to bad schools; they have little or no medical care; their life expectancy is short; they are cheated by merchants and beaten by the police; they are despised among men.

It is sometimes alleged that there is a conspiracy among the police, the merchants, the educators, the government officials, and other proprietors of the black community, a conspiracy to oppress and dehumanize black people. But this is not true in the sense that the proprietors may be said to work together to insure that blacks are kept in their places.

Yet while there is no conspiracy in this usual sense, *there is certainly a conspiracy of ideas.* The central theme of these ideas is that black people—people whose skins are not white, and who do not *act* like white people—are inferior to whites, or those who act like them, even to the point of being animals. Quite clearly this is the nature of the mental cast of the ghetto's proprietors, and its effect is the same as a conscious conspiracy.

Many years ago Gunnar Myrdal, the distinguished Swedish sociologist of American life, called the inconsistency between the democratic ideas expressed by Americans and the treatment of black people in America a "dilemma." What he failed to see is that there is no dilemma; there is no inconsistency in the American mind on matters of race. The professions of democratic values pertain to human beings, and black people are not considered human beings; *ergo* democratic values need not pertain to them. This was much the style of the first democrats, the citizen elite of the ancient Greek city of Athens. Democracy pertained to all citizens; they neglected to say that not everyone was a citizen in Athens; in fact, quite a few were slaves. Acts of oppression do strange and ugly things to the minds of the oppressors, to those who regard black people, as less than human, as well as to the minds and personalities of the oppressed.

The psychiatrists Kardiner and Ovesey state that the central problem of the black man is that he is not able to be aggressive.[12] The acts of crime and violence these men and women commit on one another in their neighborhoods bear ample witness to the inadequacy of this position. But if not the Kardiner and Ovesey position, then what? The central problem of the oppressed personality is not that its bearer is deprived and despised, nor that he accepts this condition, as Kardiner and Ovesey would have us believe. The central problem is that his rage in response to oppression is turned on himself and others that he identifies in the extension of himself into society, as like him, rather than on his oppressors.[13]

The black man in contemporary urban America has an understanding of his condition that goes far beyond what white people and most black political organizers attribute to him. He *knows* that he is oppressed and despised. He *knows* that he accepts his condition. And he is enraged. But his rage is taken out on himself, for he is confused: though

12. Abram Kardiner and Lionel Ovesey, *The Mark of Oppression* (World, 1951), pp. 304–5.

13. Kardiner and Ovesey come within a single pace of making this their central assertion. Frantz Fanon makes this a major theme in his controversial and brilliant book, *The Wretched of the Earth* (Grove Press, 1966), p. 40.

he *knows* better, he *believes* himself to be inferior. Turning on himself in acts of self-defilement, he overeats, overdrinks, and takes heroin. And turning on those like him, he robs, cheats, steals, and kills his brothers in the black community. And as he becomes caught up more and more in this life, he becomes increasingly enraged, for he knows in his very soul that the affluent white man is the enemy, and not the brother he brutalizes in the black community.

HOW CAN THE OPPRESSED SEEK IMPROVEMENTS?

Ways of bringing wayward children back into the fold do not speak to this rage and understanding. Retraining programs and bland classes in black history do not speak to the riot, to the insurrection.[14] A man does not cause an insurrection because he does not have a job; he causes it because he *knows why* he does not have a job, because he is oppressed, because he has had almost everything stolen from him, not by a conspiracy of exploitation but by a conspiracy of ideas justifying oppression, ideas featuring the black man as violent and foolish, slow and lazy, ignorant and without understanding.

The question, then, is how can the oppressed urban black peoples of America come to redirect their rage and understanding into acts of self-celebration, away from the present well-worn channels of self-destruction engendered by the American tradition of racial oppression.

14. M. T. Puryear, for example, has written a report on several facets of the present condition of American blacks. It is excellent as far as it goes, but it does not get to the heart of the matter. (See "Technology and the Negro," published by the National Urban League, New York.)

Imperfect socialization as a necessary precondition. To develop imperfectly socialized men requires leadership, not by middle-class strangers to the ghetto, but by lower-class indigenous persons. These leaders are necessarily extraordinary men, for they must be clearly identifiable as of the lower-class black community yet they must have redirected their own rage into channels no longer destructive to themselves and their neighbors but productive of alterations in the conditions of the community. They must somehow have found their way out of the trap between the knowledge that they are oppressed and the belief that they are inferior.

At home and in school socialization, both black and white children are taught that blacks are inferior. For a black child to escape this "learning," something unusual must happen to him as he is inducted into society so that he not only knows that he is oppressed, but also believes that he does *not deserve* to be oppressed.

Beyond the precondition. But imperfect socialization is not enough. Without other important events, the potential leadership in the oppressed black man may not be realized. He must develop the ability to strike back against oppression—developed through the successful pursuit of legal or illegal ways of making a living in the years following childhood. Success, even success as a criminal, fosters self-confidence and independence in thought and act.[15]

Further, there must be some precipitating incident or events providing the individual with an opportunity for action. It may be an appeal from an organization or social

15. Richard A. Cloward, "Illegitimate Means, Anomie, and Deviant Behavior," *American Sociological Review*, XXIV (1959), p. 168.

movement that speaks to his imagination and feelings, or the more complex emergence of a new understanding of oneself precipitated by another kind of incident. For the gambler like William Darden to realize that he is cheating his friends and brothers rather than his enemies is not easy to explain. For the armed robber like William Clark to come to the same kind of realization is equally difficult to explain. I am forced to fall back on the notions of strength, self-understanding, and insight in trying to explain why these men, and others like them, change their means of livelihood in the absence of a strong appeal from a social movement.

SOCIAL CHANGE AND THE INDIVIDUAL

An adequate view of social change concerns both individual and society. For the men who are the leaders of the West Side Organization, social change is a redirecting of their energies into new channels that makes them feel more comfortable with themselves. Through this kind of mobilization of self for social action, through this kind of reorientation of the self, social change comes to have the most profound meaning for individuals—and ultimately for the society in which they live.

THE VIEW OF SOCIAL SCIENCE:
OPPRESSION, SOCIAL CHANGE, AND PERSONALITY CHANGE

The view of contemporary social science (in much American writing, at least) is different from what is exemplified by the WSO.[16] It does not facilitate the consideration of

16. Obviously there are many perspectives on social analysis in the writings of contemporary social science. The "view" discussed here is

oppression, and generally, it erroneously seeks to find some neutral ground between oppressed and oppressor. This strange country of neutrality is elusive and exotic; it may not even exist. Yet in the search for it many contemporary practitioners of social science have committed sins in its name—among them the celebration (allegedly from a neutral position) of the extant social order.

The literature of contemporary social science is plentiful with studies that describe and explain things human beings *do with* one another and *give to* one another, while there are relatively few studies concerned with what human beings *do to* one another; that is, there is little concern with oppression.

For example, studies of the induction of human beings into society are labeled "studies in socialization."[17] In these enterprises social scientists study what socializers give to the socialized—what the father gives to the son, what the teacher gives to the pupil, what the school child gives to his schoolmate. But the socialization of children into societies could also be studied with emphasis on what is taken away from children in the socialization processes, with what possibilities are eliminated, with what hopes are destroyed.

This criticism may also be leveled against the literature on the "developing areas" of the world.[18] This literature

a stereotype that summarizes, and oversimplifies, some of the unfortunate tendencies in many of these perspectives.

17. One of the most celebrated works on socialization is Erik H. Erikson's *Childhood and Society* (Norton, 1963). Even Erikson takes the usual perspective. Fred I. Greenstein's work on political socialization shares this view as well; see, for example, "The Benevolent Leader: Children's Images of Political Authority," *American Political Science Review*, LIV (1960), pp. 934–943.

18. David E. Apter, among the most enlightened of the writers in this field, takes this posture in *The Politics of Modernization* (University of Chicago Press, 1965).

largely concerns itself with how nonliterate peoples may be made literate and how their economic systems may be industrialized—with emphasis on how these changes take place in the face of resistance from ancient ways of doing things. Again, the emphasis all too often is on what industrialization gives to these peoples, rather than on what it takes away if accomplished in the usual ways.

When oppression is studied, most often it is in relation to societies designated as enemies of the American people or foreign to the American way of life. Oppression is much discussed in connection with communist and socialist countries, and the questions around which research is structured ask what is taken away from the Russian people, for example, by their brand of social organization. Similarly, ways of life designated as tribal are frequently featured as oppressive. As in the case of studies of communist and socialist countries, researchers may ask how the social organization of African chiefdoms (bad) inhibit the formation of nation-states (good), in depriving (bad) Africans of the privileges of civilization (good).

But despite the fact that considering oppression in social relations and personality development has been avoided, there is much written in contemporary social science on the subject of social change.[19] Yet as rich and diverse as this genre of theoretical literature is, almost all studies in it have one common element: in their attention to changes in groups, nations, and other social aggregates, they tell us very little about the problems of the individual human being as he confronts a changing and bewildering parade of social events.

On the other hand, there is a large literature that deals

19. A useful critical review of such theories is given in J. A. Ponsioen, *The Analysis of Social Change Reconsidered* (Mouton, 1965).

specifically with changes in individuals. There are studies on attitude change and personality change and development, on psychotherapy and the social bases of mental illness, and on the social factors involved in perception, all of which provide an insight into the problems of the individual who confronts what he *perceives* to be changing social circumstances.[20] Yet this body of knowledge says very little about aggregates of human beings, let alone about whole societies or cultures.

As useful and interesting as these two perspectives on social change are, each is insufficient in itself, for neither does an adequate job of relating man to society in a rich and instructive fashion that speaks to life as we know it. Bridging this gap is a most urgent agenda item of social science. It is only in this articulation of the social and the individual perspectives on social change, and on social life generally, that social science can flower in ways that will enable it to provide the creative and constructive social criticism we so badly need. The result of the gap between individual and social perspectives on human life is that the literature of contemporary social science lacks instructive writings that would help us decide what we should do—a greater undertaking than simply telling us *what* events occur and *how* they happen. At few knots in the web of social science literature can one find a human being confronting society and society responding. In the literature taking the small view,

20. For example, Leon Festinger, *A Theory of Cognitive Dissonance* (Row, Peterson, 1957); Joseph W. Eaton, *Culture and Mental Disorders* (Free Press, 1955); Solomon E. Asch, "Effects of Group Pressure Upon the Modification and Distortion of Judgments," in *Readings in Social Psychology*, 3rd. ed., Eleanor E. Maccoby *et al.*, eds. (Holt, 1958).

one sees only the confrontation of the individual with a vague and awesome entity, society. In the literature taking the large view, we see the machinations of aggregates of human beings in which no *single* man is to be found. In either case, the literature does not guide us to what we should do, nor does it help us assess praise and distribute blame in individual behavior or in the dynamics of social orders. It seldom adequately confronts the relation between the oppressed and their oppressors.

Imperfect Socialization and the Imperfect Oppressed Personality of WSO Leaders

How have the leaders of WSO managed to escape the trap of the oppressed personality? What has happened to them that the potential of leadership has not been taken from them as they have progressed through childhood, adolescence, and early adulthood? Why are they psychologically free, while so many others remain imprisoned? The answers to these queries lie in their growth and change in childhood and adulthood socialization.

CHILDHOOD SOCIALIZATION

The leaders of the West Side Organization have managed to escape becoming ordinary Negroes; that is quite obvious from the fact of their work in the organization. Some have come to be different as the result of experiences in early childhood, while others have been changed later in life, presumably building on some childhood experience that liberated them from the normal experiences of black children in the ghettos of Chicago.

Chester Robinson, leader of WSO and the strongest man in the organization, is the closest to the ideal aberrant case of black personality development. His father and uncles did not run from a potentially violent confrontation with a gang of armed white men. Of all the major leaders of WSO, Robinson has the clearest and strongest background of imperfect training in the belief that he and all black people are inferior. Usually black children are taught by society that they are inferior—without qualification. Even as a very young child, Robinson was not taught this, but the truth. Even though he was raised in the West Side black community of Chicago under the harshest conditions, and even though his family (especially his father) was weakened by these hardships, he learned that no white man is necessarily his superior simply because he is white.

As children William Darden, William Clark, and John Crawford did not have the same kind of experiences as Robinson, though I am certain that something must have happened early in the lives of all these men to leave their minds open to the possibility of shaping successful careers in the street as hustlers, and to the possibility of political action in the style of WSO. It is probably important that both Darden and Crawford were the first-born male children in their families, which would promote the development of an independence beyond that possible for children born behind them. It is also probably important that Clark was born the last child in his very large family. Feeling ignored, he began when he was very young to turn outside the family for his social life and support.

As the eldest children, Darden and Crawford were expected to protect and look after their younger brothers and sisters, and keep them from being molested or beaten by older children, black or white. Clark, in looking outside his family, found Chester Robinson when they were both young boys. Robinson was a few years older and by example taught Clark the kind of perspective he had on matters of race. Even as small boys the two of them would purposely go places where they knew white people did not want them to go. They would go together to restaurants in the Loop (downtown Chicago) and sit down to be served what little meal they could afford—simply to be defiant, to buck the folkways that would have denied them the right even to set foot in the restaurants. (Remember this was about twenty years ago.)

As for the white people prominent in the organization, Robert Strom and Patricia Stock: Strom recalls a strong racist element in his family, set against guilt-ridden accounts of how an uncle managed to kill a black man in the South with impunity. Though it is not clear what his views on matters of race were in childhood, certainly the early alienation from some members of his family (and their racism) prepared the way for building the antiracist views of his later life. Patricia Stock was a very independent child and is an equally independent young woman. Her family did not spout the concern with racism that was part of Strom's childhood, and she was never alienated from her family. The important changes in her life that ultimately brought her to WSO did not come until much later.

All but one of these men and women had childhoods that were not normal in the context of the place their families held in American society.

ADULT SOCIALIZATION

What happened to these people after childhood that transformed them into the kinds of individuals able to do the work of a serious political organization in the black community? Beyond the disparities in childhood experiences, things even out in these lives, and similarities begin to appear that are not visible in an examination of the experiences of childhood alone. Three of the four black men, Robinson, Darden, and Clark, were successful hustlers, in contrast to Crawford, who never became quite so deeply involved in illegal pursuits, but who did become an eminent street and bar-room fighter. All four were successful, then, in different pursuits: Robinson as a marijuana salesman, Darden as a gambler, Clark as a hold-up man, and Crawford as a street fighter. From early adolescence all four were known as men who would not take anything from anybody. And now, though they are no longer deeply involved in the illegal aspects of street life, they still take nothing from no one, black or white, as they conduct the business of WSO.

All four had made attempts at achieving success through legitimate employment, with more or less success, but all four failed to make it in the straight life because the game was stacked against them. All four turned to other pursuits in which they were more successful. All four spent time in jail. All four, in short, were very much in the mainstream of life in the Near West Side community, and were successful at it. They were high-status persons in their community before there ever was a West Side Organization. In consonance with the findings of political behavior research, it is these, the high-status people of a community, who are most likely to participate in meaningful political activities. But, significantly, what is meaningful politics for Gold Coast and suburbs is oppressive for the black community. The only meaningful political action for the Near West Side, with the capacity to capture the imagination of the black and poor, is the politics of a WSO, the Deacons for Defense, and similar "no jive" organizations.

Strom and Stock both were reoriented by their educations beyond high school. Strom at Oberlin College as an English major began to contemplate moral issues and the nature of man and society, these as an outgrowth of what had troubled him as a boy in his relations with his family. And as a student at Princeton Theological Seminary he immersed himself in the intellectual life of nearby Greenwich Village, where he became enchanted with urban life. In the face of the bigotry and shortsightedness of the congregations in his first ministerial appointments in northern New Jersey, he continued seeking insight into the problems of American society by breaking his ties with the east and coming to Chicago where he became an organizer for WSO. It would be simple-minded and wrong to say that he is still trying to work out the problems incurred by the unpleasant issues raised in early childhood, but it is certain that his present concerns for the dramatic improvement of the condition of black people in America find their roots in his early years.

In contrast to his, the experience of Patricia Stock is not filled with the search for insights into the concerns of theology and philosophy. She is quite simply a professional journalist, interested in putting out a good newspaper on her own terms in a part of American society where her talents will be the most effective in promoting her values. She came to WSO almost by accident, for she probably could have found the same satisfactions in some other journalistic experience. Though she is certainly not a bigot, she is not a revolutionist either. She takes people and events as they come to her, and is very even tempered. Yet she is tough, as are all good journalists, and is not easily put on or abused.

All these men and women share certain characteristics: they are all successful, the whites at their professions of religion and journalism, the blacks at their professions of gaming and hustling. They are all sensitive, tough, and patient. They are all action-oriented, thinking always in terms of what is to be done now and in the future, rather than spinning dreams about how they wish things would be. They dream, but their emphasis is on the here and now. They are all intensely individual. Indeed, what may distinguish them from others, both black and white, is that they are unafraid to be individuals, unafraid to do different things from their fellows. And how they got this way has, for most of them, roots in the experiences of childhood.

Personality Change and Social Change—from the Perspective of the Oppressed

The perspective of the oppressed on personality change and social change begins with the intense awareness of their oppression and with the strong need to overcome it "by whatever means necessary," including possibly the use of violence. Unlike the perspective of contemporary social science, there is no quest for some middle ground of neutrality or objectivity. One must be squarely on the side of the oppressed and opposed to the oppressors. The leaders

of WSO are squarely on the side of the oppressed black
peoples of America, especially those on the Near West
Side, and opposed to all who oppress them, of whatever
color.

OPPRESSION AND THE DISTRIBUTION OF
INTELLIGENCE IN SOCIETY

The leaders of WSO are social analysts, even social scientists. They think hard about the society that confronts
them in seeking to resist the oppression to which black men
and others are subjected in America. They gather data in
their experiences finding jobs for the impoverished, handling
welfare grievances, relating to other organizations, and in
conducting the other business of WSO. Though they have
not assembled their "findings" into an "orderly body of
knowledge," what they have learned is rapidly congealing
into a perspective on life in the black community and on
American life, which is different from the perspectives of
mainstream social analysts.

Those who would turn their faces away from the bare
facts of oppression in American society would also deny
that impoverished and uneducated American black people
could be adequate social analysts; they would discredit the
social science of WSO leaders from the outset because the
black men who run WSO do not have the badges of higher
learning and respectability (among bourgeois white people,
at least) considered requisite for social criticism and analysis.

But the consideration of the effects of oppression counters
such criticisms. Oppression means that certain kinds of
people are kept from participating in high-status activities
in society—whether these activities are making a lot of

money, living in a nice place, or wearing the robes of a
cardinal or university professor. When I say that blacks
are oppressed in America, I mean, among other things, that
they are kept from participating in such high-status activities. It has been demonstrated that intelligence is not dis-
tributed with favor to any racial group in American society
or elsewhere,[21] and yet a very small percentage of black
men engage in high-status activities for which we consider
intelligence a prerequisite. Hence we must conclude that
most of the black people in America of high intelligence are
uneducated and impoverished. This is not to celebrate the
doubtful virtues of being poor; it is simply to state one of
the ugly results of oppression in America.

It is certain that there are black people (and whites) in
the American ghettos of race and poverty who, though they
have not been educated, have great insights into the society
surrounding them. What follows is a report of their thoughts
and outlooks on personality change and social change—on
social analysis generally.

LOOKING FROM THE INSIDE OUT

Most of the writing on the world of the poor and black
in American cities have been done from the view of the
middle-class social scientist or journalist, with a few precious
exceptions. What is found looking from the inside out is a
different view, one that is hightly personalized, that may
very well make a contribution to the modification of the
social sciences in a way that will link individual and aggre-
gate perspectives on social analysis. This kind of analysis is

21. Otto Klineberg, "Racial Psychology," in *American Minorities*,
Milton L. Barron, ed. (Knopf, 1957), pp. 46–47.

prescribed by writers in the sociology of knowledge, who would have us try to think about different views of the same social circumstances. They ask us to examine not only the view that middle-class social scientists bearing badges of respectability have of the black community, but also the view of the most astute of the inhabitants of the black community. It is quite certain that if the perspectives of the poor and black are ignored in thinking about how to eradicate slums and end racial oppression in American cities, no progress toward these goals may be made; indeed, no critical assessment of the worth of the goals themselves is possible.

STRESS ON CONFRONTATION OF INDIVIDUAL
WITH SOCIETY

Like the perspectives of the psychologist, those of the WSO leaders are intensely personal, stressing the confrontation of the individual with society. Yet the difference lies in *what* is thought to be confronting the individual. Where psychologists leave the orderly thinking about how society is organized to sociologists, the social scientists of WSO do not.

It is clear that many of them despise a stereotyped white man, and feature him as insensitive and cruel, ignorant, and without compassion. But they believe that there are very few who fit the stereotype. And most important, they have no clear categories to classify individual human beings, be they black or white, but operate in their relations to society on an extemporaneous, almost existentialist, basis.

They speak about categories in speeches and casual conversation (even in interviews), about what is wrong with whites and with blacks, but the way they operate in dealing with both whites and blacks does not belie any such simple categories. A black man may come into the office seeking help in finding a job. In the opening interview Robinson, who handles most of the employment operation, will quiz him only about his skills and will not ask him questions about whether or not he drinks a lot or why his clothes are dirty (if he happens to be ill-kempt). The man is seen first as an individual, and only secondarily as a member of some category: black or white, clean or dirty, skilled or unskilled. And he is seen as a member of these categories only because it is necessary in thinking about presenting him to a prospective employer. Similarly, a woman may come in seeking help with a grievance against the Cook County Department of Public Aid. She may be a known prostitute or perhaps a thief. Yet she is not considered a member of these categories; she is considered only as she presents herself at the moment —as an individual who requires assistance in what she perceives to be some difficulty she can not handle by herself. At WSO individuals are taken seriously in the way they present themselves to the organization, and these presentations of self are considered only in the context of the moment. Very little consideration is given to the reputation of the individual.

This is different from the approach practiced by clergymen and others who work in slums, who say, "I will help the addict and the prositute in spite of what they are." Implicit in the approach of WSO is the notion that what an individual *is,* he is only at the moment. What he *was* is important, but not crucial. Further, the men who work at WSO are not easily fooled. Though they are open and compassionate, they are not suckers; they are not easy prey for those who would try to get jobs through WSO they do not intend to keep.

They view society as organized consistently to oppress those who are black, but they are not so wedded to this view that they cannot always deal with human beings as individuals. The most astute of them view *any* vision of society as something to be used by one man on another to affect his view of himself. They view the predominant vision of America as an open society as something that white men have used on blacks to make them believe they are inferior and to keep them from rebelling. Equally, however, they view, at least implicitly, the image of the white man's oppression of the black man in America as a tool they can use to alter the self-image of individuals who are clients of the organization.

They see society as essentially unordered; or rather, they believe that to ask how society is ordered is to embark on a path that does not lead to further understanding of mankind. They do not engage in arguments among themselves over conflicting constructions of social reality, on conflicting ideologies. Rather, these constructions are important only in the ways they shape the individual's mind and self-conception. And so, constructions of social reality and theories about the social life of mankind are evaluated and utilized in terms of how they contribute to the dignity of black people in America. They do not ask how society is ordered, but how individuals can be made happy and dignified. And the answers they give for black individuals prescribe that they should meet oppression as it occurs, on a piecemeal basis, fighting every single oppressive act that the others, be they black or white, try to do to them. They see no systems; they draw no grandiose schemes. They think in terms of the single act of dehumanization done by one man to another. They stress the importance and value of the individual as he exists at the moment, regardless of what he has been or will be, and they support each other in the organization and its clients on this basis.

In short, *they equate social change and personality change.*

A Different Social Science?

This view of human action has far-reaching implications for the development of social science. Unlike much of contemporary American social science, it is *consciously* moral. It does not seek any neutral ground or objectivity. It says to the individual man, "I am on your side without qualification. But let us see who you are." It asks what is good and bad in each individual, and according to whose view it is good or bad. It asks who is good and helpful to the individual, and who is evil and oppressive. It does not, however, speak in categories of individuals, as black or white, weak or strong, good or evil.

It is a social science self-consciously oriented to human action—to questions of what one should do. Indeed, it is a social science that self-consciously *is* human action, an operating part of the social world itself.

The social science of WSO in taking an action-oriented position, and in coupling this awareness with a moral commitment to the individual, is not reformist, but revolutionist. For the act of unqualified commitment and the willingness to consider oppression are revolutionary in sentiment.

Yet unlike some ideas that may be labeled revolutionist

these ideas do not prescribe violence to individual or group without qualification. Since the WSO leaders do not concern themselves with systems as analytic tools (strictly speaking), they do not think in terms of destruction of the system except as altering the way some persons (the oppressors and the oppressed) deal with themselves and with one another. And that is a positive end, requiring the generation of new personalities and social visions to replace old ones, an end that may enable us to eradicate the oppression to which black people are subjected in America. Uncontrolled violence is seen as dangerous because under present conditions more is to be lost than gained through its use. What would be lost would be human lives and the dignity of black people, lost in defeat. In the unflagging emphasis on dignity, in violence or not, theirs is a gentle science that engages and nurtures the individual man, unlike much of contemporary social science in which the individual man is lost in the enchantment with groups, nations, and other categories.

Conclusion

The WSO leaders, leaders of oppressed people of Chicago's Near West Side black community, view social change and personality change differently from much of contemporary social science writings on these subjects. As in psychology, their emphasis is on the individual, but the individual is not categorized, dissected, and studied. Rather, he is engaged, nurtured, and loved. As do sociologists, they view society as ordered, but do not concern themselves with various constructions of that order except in the ways in which they impinge on the individual's thoughts about himself, and consequently, on what material benefits he receives as a result of these constructions. In this way they bridge the gap between the individual and social perspectives on the human condition that are major themes in contemporary social science—this by taking the position that the individual *is* society, that social change *is* personality change, that individual oppression *is* social oppression.

EPILOGUE

The West Side Organization is a statement of the challenge posed by black people to the American dream, a dream that for them has been a recurrent nightmare. I sense this challenge in every act of every man who is a part of the organization, for the organization requires of all who would embrace it the constant re-evaluation of the self, and the constant assertion of a new self.

As each man of WSO asserts himself in his every act, he manufactures and molds himself. And in doing so, he remakes society. In ignoring society in the intense concentration on the monstrous but minute events that confront him and to which he is impelled to react, he requires those who deal with him to change with him as he modifies himself. He requires that the policeman recognize him as a human being.

He forces the welfare official to recognize him as a threat. He compels the missionary to reassess his gods.

But his intense concern with action in his engagement with those around him is not guided by ideology. He has no beliefs that are prior to his acts, no measuring stick for human dealings. Yet he is not lost, for he has come to this moment in life, the moment when it is necessary for him to remake himself, through the encounters that constitute his life. Indeed, his new self-assertion is not so much a negation of the old self as it is a celebration of the integrity of his life and the responsibility with which he has confronted a set of circumstances posing a constant affront to his humanity.

Chester Robinson, William Darden, John Crawford, and William Clark have survived in spite of the evils heaped on them because they are poor and black. And with neither despair nor arrogance they present their survival as a challenge to America.

It is easy to misinterpret the ways they present themselves in this challenge. They are not simply saying that America is a devilish and inhuman place, nor do they prescribe the holocaust, the final calamity. To them the important thing is how human beings look upon one another and deal with one another. They are saying that white people appear as devils to black people in America, since that is the way they present themselves. They assert that all the evils of the manifold oppression of black people in this society are necessary concomitants of the image that whites have of blacks— really, not only of blacks, but of all whom they identify as "others." The men of the West Side Organization reveal and illuminate these simple but awesome facts. They reveal and illuminate the phenomena of racism and oppression.

Though the major concern of these men is not with the shape of American society in the usual sense, what they have to say is the most profound challenge to American society, because it calls on each of us to reach into the depths of our selves, to grab hold of that bit of racism in each of us (the belief in the superiority of whites is shared by whites and blacks alike in America), to examine it fully and with candor, and to remake our selves in the new understanding ensuing from these acts.

This is quite obviously a counsel of hope, of creation, for it not only entertains the possibility of escape from the ancient oppression that is America, but also offers suitable exits. The leaders of WSO are deeply committed to finding these exits. Their commitments to each other, to the people they serve, and to *mankind,* including white Americans, are serious. Their attachment to their hope is profound; they are determined to continue and expand their confrontation of racism. They are committed to doing anything necessary for the tasks they have set for themselves. These commitments may soon require them to assert their personalized revolutionary nationalism more forcefully.

The black leaders of WSO and others like them are able to ask hard questions, do difficult things, tell their truth, because they are strong. Their strength is drawn from their identity, from their culture, from who they are. In this way their acts are a celebration of their lives and those of their ancestors, who survived in the face of an evil America.

It is not so easy for the two most important white people in the organization. To celebrate their lives and those of their ancestors in the WSO context would be to celebrate racism. They are identified with the enemy. This produces extreme tension in the organization, but it becomes a creative force for both white and black because it is recognized for what it is—the heat generated by the friction of engagement with the enemy.

All recognize themselves as victims of racism and see a new responsibility in that recognition—the responsibility to remake themselves in actions that combat the manifestations of racism in others, and therefore in themselves. It becomes imperative, then, to act on welfare grievances and unemployment, and to build a viable economic basis for the black community. The whites, lacking a suitable identity on which to build, create their new identity out of these new acts. And both black and white create new beliefs out of them.

This is an achievement. As I look about in the United States at the forms the black revolt has taken. I see many efforts, like TWO and the civil rights movements, directed at issues WSO views as peripheral. I also see many efforts, like the Black Muslims, immobilized by the tension generated by the recognition of the importance of racism in America. The TWOs act, but not on what WSO views as the central issue; the Muslims identify the central issue, but do not act. WSO does both: it identifies the issue and acts on it.

This is the genius of WSO. Blacks and whites in the organization have recognized each other as enemies, but they also recognize that they have a common enemy that has set them at odds. It is irrelevant to search for the inventor of racism. It is more important to deal with the problem at hand, and that is how to combat the racist mind wherever it shows itself. If the social worker or landlord is a racist, it is imperative to eliminate his oppressive acts, and in so doing, to change him. And in confronting the racist, the black man and his white ally change and remake themselves in fighting the effects of racism on themselves, most frequently manifest in their acceptance of oppressive acts.

These challenges are difficult for all, but they offer the hope that we all can remake our selves, and that America, and all of us in it, can be re-created.

SELECTED BIBLIOGRAPHY

Social Science

Becker, Howard S., *Outsiders* (Free Press, 1963).

Cloward, Richard A., "Illegitimate Means, Anomie, and Deviant Behavior," *American Sociological Review*, XXIV (1959), pp. 164–176.

Coser, Lewis, *The Functions of Social Conflict* (Free Press, 1956).

Cruse, Harold, *The Crisis of the Negro Intellectual* (William Morrow, 1967).

Erikson, Erik H., *Childhood and Society*, 2nd ed. (Norton, 1963).

Fanon, Frantz, *The Wretched of the Earth* (Grove Press, 1966; first published in French, 1961).

Kardiner, Abram and Lionel Ovesey, *The Mark of Oppression* (World, 1951).

Keil, Charles, *Urban Blues* (University of Chicago Press, 1966).

Kitagawa, Evelyn M., and Karl E. Taeuber, eds., *Local Community Fact Book: Chicago Metropolitan Area 1960* (Chicago Community Inventory, University of Chicago, 1963).

Laing, R. D., *The Politics of Experience* (Pantheon, 1967).

Milbrath, Lester W., *Political Participation* (Rand McNally, 1965).

Ponsioen, J. A., *The Analysis of Social Change Reconsidered* (Mouton, 1965).

Ross, Murray G., *Community Organization* (Harper and Row, 1955).

Silberman, Charles E., *Crisis in Black and White* (Random House, 1964).

Research Methods

Berger, Peter L., and Thomas Luckmann, *The Social Construction of Reality* (Doubleday, 1966).

Bruyn, Severyn T., *The Human Perspective in Sociology* (Prentice-Hall, 1966).

Biographies and Essays

Brown, Claude, *Manchild in the Promised Land* (Macmillan, 1965).

Cleaver, Eldridge, *Soul on Ice* (McGraw-Hill, 1968).

Jones, LeRoi, *Home* (William Morrow, 1966).

Memmi, Albert, *The Colonizer and the Colonized* (Orion, 1965; first published in French, 1957).

Wright, Richard, *The Outsider* (Harper, 1953).

X, Malcolm, *The Autobiography of Malcolm X* (Grove Press, 1964).

X, Malcolm, *Malcolm X Speaks*, George Breitman, ed. (Grove Press, 1966).